Christian Darley was born in 1962 and graduated from the University of Oxford with a degree in Classics. She was awarded a scholarship by the French Government to attend the École de Mime Corporel Dramatique de Paris. She also trained in Pantomime Blanche with Ella Jaroszewicz at the Théâtre Magenta, Paris, and worked with Adam Darius at the Mime Centre, London, and with Christian Mattis in Zurich. Hand in hand with this went intensive work with Monika Pagneux and Philippe Gaulier, and residential courses with Jonathan Kay, Dominique de Puy and Théâtre du Mouvement.

In 1993 she was appointed to the Department of Movement at the London Academy of Music and Dramatic Art, specialising in Movement Theatre, becoming Masterclass leader in 2001. She founded her Movement Laboratory in 2003. Throughout this time she was working with LAMDA students on productions, some of which are referred to in this book. Amongst many freelance assignments as movement director she worked for Sturdy Beggars and the Oxford Stage Company, and on *Footfalls* and *Rockaby* for the 1999 Bergen International Festival, *My Dad's a Birdman* for the Young Vic and *The Tempest* for the National Theatre (both 2003).

She also conducted movement workshops in the community and for theatre in education, and within contexts of residential teaching, special needs and prisons.

She died aged forty-six in 2008, just after completing the first draft of this book.

Christian Darley

The Space to **MOVE**

Essentials of Movement Training

Christian Darley

Edited by Linda Baker, Dictynna Hood and Sue Mitchell

NICK HERN BOOKS
London
www.nickhernbooks.co.uk

A Nick Hern Book

The Space to Move
first published in Great Britain in 2009
as a paperback original by Nick Hern Books Limited,
14 Larden Road, London W3 7ST

Cover designed by Peter Bennett
Cover photograph by Gonzalo Aguilar León

Typeset by Nick Hern Books, London
Printed and bound in Great Britain by
CPI Antony Rowe, Chippenham, Wiltshire

A CIP catalogue record for this book is available
from the British Library

ISBN 978 1 84842 024 3

For Dictynna Hood

Contents

Publisher's Note   ix
Editors' Note   xi

Beginnings   xiii
Introduction   1

Chapter One—*Starting the Work*   5
Chapter Two—*Musicality: Being* à l'Écoute   13
Chapter Three—*The Business of Relaxation*   19
Chapter Four—*Getting the Best Out of Technique*   29
Chapter Five—*Play and the Importance of Suspension*   50
Chapter Six—*Animal Work*   59
Chapter Seven—*Contact Work*   80
Chapter Eight—*The Actor's Voice*   100
Chapter Nine—*Musicality and Visual Spacing*   124
Chapter Ten—*The Mystery of Music and Props*   145
Chapter Eleven—*Pastoral Care*   156
Chapter Twelve—*Working with Children*   159
Chapter Thirteen—*Working with the Army*   169

In Conclusion   177
Afterword—*And Another Thing…*   179
Appendix—*Exercises*   180

On Working with Christian…   186
    Richard Armitage, Samuel Barnett,
    Dominic Cooper and Félicité du Jeu

Index   190

Publisher's Note

I had just read the first draft of this book when news came that Christian Darley had died. The book has been prepared for publication by three of her friends and colleagues, named as editors on the title page. I am extremely grateful to them—and have enjoyed working with them.

Nick Hern

Editors' Note

Christian was frustrated that she was unable to teach any more because of illness, so Dictynna Hood, with whom Christian often collaborated, suggested that she write a book about her teaching.

The book took shape over the period of two years from 2004: at first as a series of responses that Christian wrote longhand to questions faxed or sent to her by Dictynna. The book was then typed up by Daphne Mitchell.

A couple of months before she died in 2008, Christian invited Sue Mitchell, Linda Baker and Dictynna to edit *The Space to Move* for her. Sue trained with Decroux in Paris. Linda has taught drama for thirty-eight years. Dictynna is a director. Like Christian, Dictynna studied Classics and has collaborated with her on three Greek plays.

Peter James, Head of LAMDA, approached Nick Hern with the typescript.

*

As editors, we have changed some of the ordering of the book to make it flow more clearly, and we have adapted some chapter headings. We are delighted that Christian was able to write this wonderful book, and that her work can now leap off the page and continue to inspire others as it has inspired us.

Christian had a rare insight that her chosen editors would work and play well together—and we have!

Linda Baker, Dictynna Hood and Sue Mitchell

Beginnings

John Barton's *Henry V* at Stratford in 1971 when I was nine. Sitting down in the auditorium, people chatting, actors wandering about onstage, casually choosing casual costumes off rails and slowly pushing the rails to clear an empty space. Spectators carry on talking. Why are the actors dressing on-stage? I felt I was prying, but also rather enjoying young men with nice legs changing their trousers. Suddenly an actor finishes buttoning his shirt and walks—a totally different walk—into the space. Lights change. Transformation! Theatre with the snap of the fingers, but also a walk.

When I was eleven I gave up ballet. I'd done Grade 4 and wasn't going to be a ballet dancer. Thanks to growing up in a college with plenty of spacious rooms, I would put on the tape recorder and dance whenever I could. It was a drug. But I loved to play and was drawn more and more to theatre and the grandeur of opera. At seventeen, I saw *Les Enfants du Paradis*, and this classic French film made sense of everything I was interested in. Jean-Louis Barrault's sublime playing of the mime Deburau, 'Baptiste' in the film, woke me up to the vast possibilities of movement for an actor, before the actor even utters a word onstage. So I went to Paris, and under the terrifying eye of Ella Jaroszewicz of the Tomaszewski Pantomime Theatre, studied Pantomime Blanche and illusionary mime. Ella, tough as old boots, worked us like dogs until we could dismiss the technique and play. Then she became beautiful. I returned to England and university, in love with Paris, in love with mime, but acutely aware I'd only touched on a vast world that moved.

Introduction

This is a book for actors, directors, students and teachers. It is for anyone interested in looking at what it means to have the space to move, and how that space to move directly affects the way an individual actor or group performs, be it on the stage or in the studio or in the classroom, or anywhere else. This is not a textbook or a list of exercises, nor is it an academic exposition of movement techniques. It is a look at the process of movement training as it happens on the floor and how that process is a process of play.

I like to imagine that process as something akin to the inflation of an enormous balloon: from the half-hour before the curtain goes up, for example, until the last curtain call, a balloon has slowly been inflated by every member of the company. The balloon, fully inflated, will take off, not necessarily in the direction expected, but nevertheless it will take off. The process of a rehearsal or workshop also has this balloon-like quality. That is the ideal. But there are good shows and bad shows, good rehearsals and bad, when the darned balloon doesn't have a chance of inflating: X didn't show up, Y 'doesn't do' company warm-ups, there *are* no company warm-ups, Z was late, the actors are out of sorts, there was a bad review, the studio is gloomy, and cold… Hundreds of reasons or just a few, but each is a little pin slow-puncturing the balloon. It cannot take off. There is no movement into a new space, the play space where things happen.

Over the years the greater part of my work as a movement director has been concentrated on what makes a rehearsal work, what allows an actor to transform totally, what is the process happening in a company when the balloon lifts off… actually, what *is* a company for that matter? After taking a long look at my work in professional theatre, my teaching work at LAMDA and my work with individuals outside the profession, my odd successes and dreadful failures, I realise that the answers lie in the creation of an atmosphere: an atmosphere in which extraordinary work can evolve. My job was to promote that atmosphere by recognising the need for space in both the actor and the group that he or she is part of, space in which to be fully present in order to work; in this business, that means the space to play.

Movement Training

Both inside and outside the acting profession there has been a tendency to see movement as an 'extra' ('Oh, we don't need any movement in this show…'), something you can be 'good' or 'bad' at ('Can I sit this one out, Christian, I'm no good at movement?'). Today, theatre schools understand the vital role of movement in actor training, yet 'movement', 'pure movement', 'movement for actors' can still remain an elusive business, even with the straightforward 'mastery of movement' as a common goal. This is simply because movement is not a set discipline as in ballet or in fight. There is no laid-down technique called 'movement', and thank heavens for that! How can there be a technique set in stone for both Maia, a professional ballet dancer for five years who now wishes to become an actor, and for Tom, slightly overweight, who arrives at drama school with a horror of anything 'physical'?

The directors and teachers of movement in the theatre world come from many different backgrounds, from ballet to Decroux, Laban, Lecoq and Grotowski to name a few, and we adapt and turn our training inside out to meet the needs of the actor in front of us. As a result, the business of movement training is constantly growing and developing in its common, fundamental purpose: enabling the actors before us to play, and to play well. Most of us movement directors are, or have been, performers, and this bringing of bodies together to play is what unites and identifies us.

A Note on Words

In this book I have used certain words again and again: 'awareness', 'noticing', 'listening' and 'musicality', words often used by practitioners like myself. These words explain a process: when we explore them, we can begin to feel the flesh, the physical activity whence they get their meaning. The French word, '*écouter*' ('to listen') is derived from the business of scouting, spying and seeking out information. It is describing the business of being alert, a body in total engagement. The Latin for 'I notice' is '*animadverto*', literally, 'I turn my soul towards', an activity of total engagement. 'Awareness' is derived from Old Saxon, '*giwar*'('being on one's guard', 'watchful') and in Middle English this came to be identified with being conscious, being sensible, a body engaged in the here and now. And what of 'engagement' itself, with its roots in Latin and Old French, meaning 'pledging' and 'committing'?

The words describing tremendous physical activity have arisen from exactly those activities themselves, activities of the flesh. But over time, much of the flesh has been lost. We tend to understand words such as 'listening', 'awareness', and 'noticing' as words to do with the head, eyes, ears and brain. They stop at the neck.

It is my hope in this little book to bring back some of the lost flesh to these words: to show how, on the studio floor, in the classroom, in the working space, it is the body that does the listening and the noticing, the body that has the awareness, the body, even, that does the thinking, has the inspiration and has the judgement. Above all, it is the body that has the imagination, an enormous imagination, that will out, given the right space to move.

All the names of actors mentioned have been changed. Should anyone recognise him or herself, then I can only stress that they taught me much more than I taught them.

Chapter One

Starting the Work

A New Start

The group may know each other very well or they may have only exchanged words of greeting in the changing rooms, but this won't necessarily alter what I am going to do with them. Students arrive with a variety of baggage: exhaustion, 'late night last night', row with girlfriend, washing machine in shared flat exploded (a frequent happening it seems), nerves, fear of failure, terror of this thing called 'movement', boredom with 'movement', a clear conviction that 'movement' is a waste of time, or huge keenness with notebooks at the ready to get as much info as possible on 'movement', that important accessory to acting. You get everything tumbling through those doors, but all of them are ready in their different ways to go through their three or four hours with me. But what does this 'ready' mean? If you asked them all, 'Are you ready to begin?' (like the old *Listen with Mother*'s 'Are you sitting comfortably?'), they would probably all answer 'yes', and you could launch into a talk about the programme for the session, its place in theatre, etc., or simply dive into a name game to break the ice or a game of 'Tag' to get the energy going. This will probably make them readier to begin, but do they know how this has happened and isn't it just a case of being warmer? '*Rechauffement*.' The French word has the sense of getting warm again. Do we miss something crucial in our simplified 'warm-up'?

There are hundreds of very good books on acting, on movement, on training and exactly where and how the study of movement, the art of movement, the role of movement fits into that training. 'Our body is our instrument': we know that old and very true cliché; we need to fine tune the instrument, make it serve us, feel comfortable and whole in ourselves. More clichés, and very laudable and sensible ones they are, too. We are after the integration of mind and body: a physical actor who is available to the work in hand, where he is completely able to inhabit not simply another character, but another world...

Where to Begin

Lots of fine tuning is required: stretch classes, Alexander Technique, Feldenkrais, Pilates, mime, mask, acrobatics, fencing and stage combat... Much to do and many skills to be learned. The student's body is a blank canvas on which to graft these fabulous techniques. Or is it?

For the teacher of movement, what does any of this mean when standing in front of a group of ten, twenty or thirty new students? How to begin this tuning and pruning business? What does the teacher want at the end of this three-hour session, for example? The students may have expectations, but they won't be consistent. They can't be. The teacher can and should have expectations because they will inform him or her how to direct the class. At the end of three hours, one wants to have achieved a working group—i.e. a group that can work together to produce work that elevates the work of each individual. Let's call this new group an 'ensemble', and we can return to the 'tuning-up' analogy. The 'en' bit of 'ensemble' is crucial: the students are 'in' something together and this will totally influence how they learn whatever it is you are trying to teach them. Where there is an ensemble there is shape, and where there is shape there is also form and sense. The student is not on his or her own and is consequently adapting to and being moulded by the ensemble that he or she is also moulding by simple reason of being a part of it. They are being tuned, and it is worth remembering that it is a whole orchestra that tunes up: the instruments do not tune up in separate rooms before meeting.

Arranging the Class

My little girl has a bag of beads. When she plays with them she starts by emptying them onto the floor. To look at them properly she will sort them, move them around and finger them—move them into a place where they seem to be seen better, and to their advantage. Then, this done, an idea pops up for a necklace, or a game or simply a pattern. The beads can be seen and their possibilities are evident and exciting.

The new bunch of students coming into the space are like the beads pouring out of the bag. You might give them an instruction ('Find a space facing this way'), and you will be flooded with physical information that cannot be read—and this could well be after you have done a name game, introductions, etc. You cannot teach a technique if the bodies in space are giving out peculiar information. And they are bodies. Students do not have bodies that need to learn movement, they are bodies that move and need to know that! You would not embark on an explanation of quantum mechanics in a pub on a Saturday night to all and sundry. It is not the appropriate space. Those present might love such a lecture, but somewhere else—where their bodies would be in a different space.

It is the same in teaching movement. Are the students literally in the right space to learn whatever it is you wish them to learn? Look at where they are in space. People like to be with their friends, people like to hide, people get too close to each other, there is not enough intelligent and safe space around them. There are always some trying to creep up the back wall, no space behind them, looking as though they have indeed been left behind. You can move them, but it's much better to encourage them to find a space they feel drawn to. Persist: they may have shuffled about a bit. Tell them the space is like a magnet. Where is the space that holds them, that attracts them? Don't be content just to go somewhere else. There will be a place where you function better. A functioning body is one that has a relationship with the space around it. Imagine how carefully you would have to arrange twenty radios in a room so that you maximised clarity and reception and minimised interference. We are much more sophisticated yet more neurotic than radios, and consequently need more arranging.

Next...

Once in a good place, it is time to allow the student to take charge. It's no good saying 'Feel your feet on the floor' or 'Locate any tension in the body'—the instruction is just too big. Students have to be taught to feel. 'Feel' is a limited word in English. '*Sentir*' in French covers 'feel', 'taste', 'smell', 'think' and 'notice'. 'Notice' would be a better word here, or 'observe'. None of us are very good at noticing how to feel, but we can all imagine things and make pictures in our heads. I remember Monika Pagneux asked us as students to imagine what a print of our feet on a piece of paper would look like. This is a good place to start. I suggest the students imagine they have blue paint on the undersides of their feet. What do the prints look like? Where is there a lot of ink? Where are the white patches? Is the right foot different from the left? The student, eyes closed, observes his or her print and memorises it. Now we have a starting point. I could choose any number of exercises at this point, but maintaining the concentration and staying in this space is important with a new group. They are safe to concentrate on themselves.

I often use the following exercise at this point:

The Pendulum

Keep the eyes closed and very gently sway from side to side like the pendulum of a clock. Slow and small, keeping the surface of the feet on the ground. Does the body fall more easily to the right or the left? A 'Brain Gym' expert would have reasons for this, but at this stage all that is important is to notice. If a student is asked to understand (or asks to understand) what is happening, then the energy will be blocked and the exercise rendered useless.

Then observe your breathing—is it something that is happening in time to the movement or totally independent of it? Don't change anything—just notice. Then move the body gently forwards and backwards, always keeping the surface of the feet on the ground.

Now, imagining there is a pen sticking out of the top of the head, gently rotate the whole body so the pen can draw a small circle on the ceiling.

Repeat the whole process, making the movements slightly larger. The atmosphere in the studio usually becomes quiet, but only if this exercise is not rushed. Still keeping the eyes closed, come to a standstill. Look at the print of the feet in the mind's eye. Has anything changed?

Most will notice a large change and all reactions will be different. The only useful thing to say is to remind the students that when the clock stops, the pendulum, thanks to gravity, rests perpendicular to the floor. We each have our own perfect perpendicularity, our own perfect posture if you like, but it has to be re-found. The students will now have felt a change, albeit very small. Until they begin to learn to 'feel'—to 'sentir'—in this very small way, they will not know how much there is to feel. This is the very beginning of understanding what it is to be in a group.

Quite often there is someone who feels no change in their print subsequent to the exercise. This is not because they are an insensitive brute, but usually because there is overtension in the muscles due to overexercise or general uptightness. Then I move to another exercise. It is very important that this person feels a difference in the very next exercise.

Centring

Flipper Feet

1. Stand with your feet parallel, six inches apart, eyes closed.

2. Notice, as in *The Pendulum* exercise, any differences between the two feet. Is one flatter on the ground than the other? Do you lean on one more than the other? Which foot would you stand on for ten minutes if you had to? Do you know? Now place an imaginary ruler across the hips and the line of the eyes. Is the ruler parallel to the floor or does it tilt? Notice.

3. Imagine you have a huge, rubber diver's flipper on your right foot. Now open your eyes and walk about with this right flipper. You have to throw the right leg forward and the 'flipper' slaps the floor. Do not stamp or hit the floor; this is a loud slap and the thigh should wobble a little. The knee is not bent when the leg arrives on the floor. Walk about the room and gradually speed up a little.

4. Stop. Feet parallel again and eyes closed. Compare the two feet and ask yourself the same questions as in the second stage, above. Pay special attention to the line of the eyes. Does one eye feel higher or lower than the other?

5. Repeat using the left leg. Close your eyes and observe the changes.

6. Put two little flippers on and move about as fast as you can. Stop, and without closing the eyes, observe the intensity of the focus.

∗

Balloons in Armpits

1. Walk about the room and consider your size in relation to those around you and the space between yourself and the ceiling.

2. Imagine that in each armpit there is a deflated balloon.

3. Breathing in on the count of five, the balloons inflate, opening the chest and lifting the arms. Walk about the room as you do this. The balloons deflate on the count of five and the chest slumps forward. Let the head drop forward. Keep walking while you inflate and deflate the balloons about ten times.

4. Now inflate the balloons to the count of six: two counts to reach a middle point, two counts in the middle point, two counts to reach super inflation. Two counts to return to the middle point, two counts to stay in the middle point and two to deflate completely. Repeat the process about five times.

5. On the fifth deflation, remain in the middle point and breathe and walk normally. Notice the difference between your original way of walking and this one in relation to the space.

Running

(NB. This exercise should never be done right at the beginning of a session.)

1. In pairs, run around the room in the largest circle possible. Start with your arms lifted high over your head, and your head lifted to gaze at your hands. Shoulders down and sternum lifted.

2. Halfway round the circle the head drops forward (floppy) as do the arms. The body is pitched forward, but the running continues at the same pace. Take care to keep the head relaxed.

3. When the circle has been completed, return to the first stage. There is no middle state between the first and second stages.

4. After each pair has completed the circle four or five times, go from the 'high state' to your normal run. Notice how you can continue running indefinitely, and also notice that not only are you running in step with your partner but that the whole group

is running in step. (One of my students at LAMDA, always apologetic and angry at his, as he saw it, lack of athleticism, carried on running for fifteen minutes after this exercise, giving us the speech he had had to prepare for his voice class: clear, open and with no hint of breathlessness.)

Both *Balloons in Armpits* and *Running* work on the same principle as *The Pendulum*: the body has to go out of its normal range to re-find its centre.

Chapter Two

Musicality: Being à l'Écoute

When actors are truly living their roles we say they are good actors: they are 'in the moment'. When good actors are able to listen to their fellow actors totally in the moment and totally without judgement, then you will have a good play. If this is supported by a technical team that is listening to the play, you will have a good production. If the players are generous enough to remember they are playing to an audience, you will have theatre.

A student actor arrives at rehearsal keen to work. The question is not so much 'Are they going to be any good?', but 'Are they ready to play?' And because playing is not something that usually happens in isolation, the next queston is 'Is the group that they are working in ready to play?' The answer is almost always 'no' at this juncture. But when the group is ready to play, each member is *à l'écoute* of the other, of the time and space and of the action. When you have this level of listening, the work flows.

Être à l'Écoute

We are always telling our acting students: 'Be aware of what you are doing.' This is easy to say, but what does it actually mean for the poor bugger who was up all night learning lines, or working behind a bar or drinking in front of it? Ask your student or group of students to take a chair and move it from A to B. Repeat the process eight or ten times. You will probably be aware of that dreadful sound you get when the school bell goes—scraping, banging, etc.—tired bodies, fed-up students and even more fed-up chairs. Now ask them to know where the chair is going, where exactly is B? When they know where B is, ask them to move it to B over a period of five to eight minutes. This is work; the body is going very, very slowly, every muscle is involved. It is a struggle, but they must not speed up. There must be no staccato, no pause. To look at, there is absolute control yet it is very hard. It is one of the most moving things to watch. When they have finished, there is no rest: they must move the chair from A to B eight times at top speed. Then rest. Now move the chair at normal speed. There is no noise, no scraping. It is a harmonious movement and the body moves with all its parts in connected fluidity to encompass the chair, to bring the chair into its orbit, if you like. The chair is respected, and if this sounds pretentious, then let's say the movement is now bearable for both actor and observer. The actor has experienced the work of the moment in every part. He is full, and therefore ready to act.

*

In the summer of 2001 I was movement director of Aeschylus's *Persai* at LAMDA. The play is remarkable for its absence of plot. Nothing really happens: the characters sit about waiting for bad news, and then they get it. The director created a remarkable show that dealt with the drama of waiting. On the second or third rehearsal, prior to warm-up, he had all the men, twenty or so (there were thirty actors in total), walk along the length of the hall we were working in, one by one, open a door at the end, and go out. Why? That is not a good question to ask directors. More to the point, was it bearable? Absolutely not, and that was no fault of the director's. The men stomped their way across the floor, went through the door and slammed it. One of the most horrible things I've seen students do. 'I know this can work, Christian.' The director is frustrated. This is where it is a bit of a Pygmalion job being a movement director, but consequently incredibly exciting. The director has an image. I don't have it. The director is rather brilliant so there is no need for me to doubt it is a splendid image. I simply have to help him get it. 'Give me half an hour,' I ask. 'As much as that?' We eyeball each other and he goes off and has a coffee.

I get the actors to walk, on their heels, toes, pushing off on the balls of the feet, feeling a springboard under the balls of their feet. What happens in the sternum when you do this, in the eyes? What happens in the sternum and the eyes when you lose the springboard, when you walk, engaging the heels only? How much less do you notice around you? Alternate between springboard and heels—find the middle way by going to the extremes, because only then is the middle way actually a middle way. What about the distance between the top of the head and the ceiling? Is there any space there?

The students keep walking, now with heels only, now pushing off and springing forward. Their antennae are out. We return to the original instruction. Now, when one student has passed through the fatal door, there is no real choice for the next in line. His body is listening, has listened to what has happened in the space as a result of the previous walk. He is now the next instrument to join the symphony and his action is a musical response. Now there is theatre because at last the spectator can dream a bit, be caught up in the flow of a seemingly repeated action, instead of thinking, 'How many more to go through that fucking door!!' The director's idea was pure genius.

*

In the final act of Verdi's *Rigoletto*, there is a quartet: Gilda is outside the tavern with her father Rigoletto. They overhear the Duke making love to Maddalena, the tavern keeper's daughter. The Duke has already raped Gilda, but she loves him. Rigoletto is bent on revenge on her behalf. Four characters, miles apart in their hopes and intentions, each has a different song, yet heard together in the tapestry of the quartet, we can fully appreciate the differences—the pleasure of one not diminishing, but enhancing the pain of another. Four characters privately expressing their own thoughts, yet we feel them all. The scene from *Rigoletto* marks a crisis point in the action of the play. It is in Act III, the final act of the tragedy of the protagonists. But how do we get that incredible gulf of emotions between four characters (who don't even all know each other in the play) to hit us hard, at the same instant, when they are onstage together? Certainly it is not a question of speaking, as they can't possibly speak at the same time and be understood. Is this something you can only achieve in opera? (In classical ballet, hardly ever.) Is this because the eye takes in less than the ear? I don't think so. It is more a question of musicality. So, how does musicality provide the answer?

When I directed Euripides's *Iphigeneia in Aulis* at LAMDA in 2003, what interested me was the situation of a large number of people stuck on a seashore waiting for the wind to change so they could sail to Troy. I had thirty actors. How to enjoy their differences? How to observe an army with a shared intention and the different personalities behind that intention? Was this necessary anyhow? In the quartet in *Rigoletto*, the musical form lays the soul of each singer bare. All characters are very vulnerable at this point. Morality is not an issue— the moment is about our response to this vulnerability. Could I achieve something similar with my actors?

Each member of the chorus had a 'thing', something peculiar to them for passing the time on the beach, whether it was building castles of cards or drawing in the sand or whatever.

The show opened with them all engrossed in their activity of 'passing time'. There were the sounds of the objects used on the floor, the sounds of the occasional gesture of impatience, a stamp, etc. We spent a great deal of time listening to each other, contact work, eyes-closed work in many different sensing exercises, until each cast member was utterly attuned to the group. Then each movement's potential musicality had to be understood: if an actor, playing cards, made a sudden movement of impatience, how did that affect the 'private' games of the rest? Each private tune, if you like, each actor's choice of play here on the beach, had to be connected spatially and musically with all the rest in order for it to be seen. For example, a single, slight impatient gesture would affect the whole scene in a very subtle way.

As the play continued, we kept coming back to this scene up until the moment where the Messenger describes the sacrifice of Iphigeneia. Clytemnestra is motionless against the backdrop of the army. The difference in the army is that now they are packing up their games, they are getting ready to go. We have seen their vulnerability in their little waiting rituals, now we see each facing the expedition and war, but still they are chaps with cards or toy soldiers. All were very quiet, but their continued musical listening to each other at this point provided the orchestration of the whole: we were able to listen to the Messenger's description of the sacrifice, but also it was possible to watch thirty different actors and take in their thirty different responses to the speech, as well as observe Clytemnestra's enormous grief and sense of betrayal.

∗

It was possible to achieve what opera can do in a quartet or quintet, but only by making the actors hear and feel how the tying of one actor's shoelace onstage had a bearing on how another drew in the sand, how another entered the stage, and when another chose to speak. All the actors were *à l'écoute* of each other. That is musicality in a nutshell and I shall return to it in Chapter Nine.

Chapter Three

The Business of Relaxation

People who don't know each other very well and are unfamiliar with any kind of body work don't much take to lying on the floor. The floor is usually hard, for a start. Mats help, but mats are never to be had when you really need them in an institution, and, unless they are pretty new, can be rather revolting and unpleasant. Mats that are regularly renewed are ideal, but this is costly. Lying on the floor in an unknown group is scary, and if you don't believe me, then lie on the floor and remember a time when you felt somewhat apprehensive, e.g. at a new school or at a job interview. Cross your ankles and fold your arms over your chest while remembering. Now how would you feel if I told you to uncross your arms and legs and, worse, turn your palms to the ceiling?

Mind you, this is a common-enough instruction in acting, dance, yoga and movement classes of almost any kind: 'Lie on the floor on your backs, arms by your sides, palms facing the ceiling and relax!' Getting a student to relax is key to their understanding of the tool they are dealing with, i.e. the body. In voice training, unless the student can feel what a relaxed body is, compared with one that is carrying tension, he or she cannot even begin to feel the capacity there is for breath and breath control. Put simply, until the body has learned that it can let go of muscles, it doesn't appreciate that it has muscles to relax. It is in some way deaf: it cannot hear what it needs in order to work efficiently. It is deaf to its potential.

Students must feel comfortable on the floor as early as possible in their training. The floor needs to be a good place to be. This sounds terribly obvious, but we are encouraged to stand on our own two feet very early (it's called 'development'); playgrounds these days are designed to cushion us against the possibility of falling, climbing frames have been removed in case we fall... Compared with twenty years ago, children have knees remarkably unscathed, which is good, but it also means we don't like falling, giving in to the ground. The ground has become a little bit dangerous. I ask the students to lie on the floor in the studio. It's sprung, clean and warm.

> 'Er, Christian, if we are on the floor, shouldn't we have our knees up, feet on the floor and a couple of telephone directories under our heads?'
>
> 'Why?'
>
> 'Well, that's what we do in an Alexander lesson when we are lying on the floor.'
>
> 'This isn't an Alexander lesson.'
>
> 'Right. But isn't it bad for us to lie on the floor?'
>
> 'Nope.'

It seems alarmingly 'seventies' to talk about 'having a good relationship with the floor', but actually, this is vital for the student of theatre. The floor is a place of discovery, and relaxation: proper relaxation leads to discovery. The floor is also a shared space where the concentrated focus of the group builds energy. It is very good to relax in your own room, alone, but it usually takes twice as long and is often not as effective as relaxing in a group. There is simply less energy, and the energy there is, is self-created which can impede relaxation.

I am not going to write a list of relaxation exercises here. There are plenty, excellently documented in many theatre books, and I would suggest Patsy Rodenburg's *The Right to Speak* (Methuen), which beautifully sets out and explains the process of relaxation. Rather, I am interested in what the student does prior to a relaxation exercise. The first few times I work with a new bunch of actors or students and we have to lie on the floor, I keep them busy:

> 'Keep your socks on; keep a jumper on if you are cold; if there are mats available, use them...'

The mats are not so much for comfort, unless the floor is particularly hard and cold, as for giving the student a boundary: their own specific, unencroachable space. I let them lie however they like.

> 'Notice if you wish to cross your ankles or cross your arms over your chest. That's fine. Now uncross your legs and turn your palms to the ceiling. Is that comfortable?'

Many do not like it, especially the rugby and football-playing lads whose muscles consider tension the norm.

> 'Go back to lying in whatever position is comfy for you.'

I leave the group there for a few minutes. There is a bit of tossing and turning. After a while some ankles uncross... Time, plenty of time is crucial for the body to feel safe on the floor, and only when it feels safe will it have the freedom to release. We are not there yet.

Now I ask the group to lie with some space between their feet, arms by their sides and palms facing the ceiling. Telling them to 'breathe deeply and *relax*' isn't usually very helpful at this stage. In fact, relaxation should be renamed 'relax-action': it is an active process necessary to produce the inaction we understand as relaxation. People go for massages or to a jacuzzi to 'relax', let go. 'That feels so good' is something we commonly say of our relaxation methods, but we are not required to examine what exactly it is that feels good. 'It' provides a break from one sort of stress or another that will release us until we need the break again. 'Let me get through this, then I'll relax,' we say. The students have to relax *before* they get busy. So, back to them:

> 'Imagine you are lying on the floor on a white sheet of paper. Covering the underside of your body is dark-blue ink. What kind of print are you making on the paper? Notice the heels: is one pressed into the floor harder than the other? Is there more of one calf on the floor than the other? Is any part of either thigh touching the floor? What about the buttocks? Is one flatter than the other or, rather, does your pelvis seem to tilt slightly? Does any of your lower back make a mark on the paper?'

We move up the body observing how the print comes out on its white sheet of paper. 'Don't change anything, just observe.' We end with the head: 'Does the head seem to be tilted very slightly to one side?' ('Dunno.')

> 'Gently turn the head from one side to the other and notice if it moves more easily in one direction. Now, keeping your eyes closed, look at the print you have made. Take a mental snapshot of it. Memorise it.'

Next, I ask the students to do a series of very small exercises, for example:

Knee Circles

1. Lying on the floor, draw your knees up so your feet are securely planted on the floor. Notice how your lower back makes greater contact with the floor in this position.

2 . Drop your right knee onto your chest and start drawing very tiny circles with your knee, as though drawing a circle on the ceiling. Go slowly: perhaps you are describing a clockface, so be sure not to miss out any of the numbers. Keep the circles small and very, very slow.

3. Now the knee is moving slowly, describe a circle with your nose at the same time as the knee circle. Let your neck and head move freely, but, again, it is a very small movement. Feel a sense of connection between the movement of head and knee.

4. Stop (never go on for more than a couple of minutes). Relax arms and legs along the floor. Compare the print you are making now on the floor to your original snapshot. Has anything changed?

The feedback is varied: 'One leg feels longer than the other' (usually the leg that has been rotating, but not always), 'My right leg feels lighter/heavier', 'My right leg is longer', My right foot is more turned out…' It goes on. We are not looking for a specific result here, more we are acknowledging that a tiny circular movement has produced change—and a comfortable one at that. We do the other leg and relax. The prints are changing. No one wants to cross their legs any more. They are beginning to feel internal connection on a very small scale, and how comfortable it can be on the floor. They notice that one side of the body may be more responsive than the other. A great deal of yawning, burping, eye-watering erupts. As the body releases its muscles there is both a release of energy and craving for oxygen. This process is awakened through movement.

Awareness Through Movement (Thorsons) is the title of Moshe Feldenkrais's superb book in which this exercise has its origins. It is about turning, through action, our powers of listening and observation inside ourselves: mind into matter, yes, but awareness is what is being cultivated. Willpower has no place here: there is no choosing to ignore a tight neck or sore lower back. The exercises allow the body to yield, to give way, so the muscles can be felt as part of a bigger picture where body parts work through cooperation rather than conflict.

I do a small series of these very small exercises—not more than two or three. Today I concentrate on the legs. Tomorrow I work on the hips. It has to be slow and small. It is like learning any skill in that it has to come gradually; discovering the tools the students have to work with takes time. Gradually they discover the means of effectively working on themselves. Again the old chestnut: the more the body learns to feel, the more there is to feel—and the body's 'feeling' possibilities are quite extraordinary!

If you are working on very deep relaxation as is often necessary, especially prior to animal or contact work, then it is important to consider where you wish the student's energy to be after the exercise; where it is going to. A person roused from very deep relaxation can be disorientated, wobbly and tired. Getting students to yawn, stretch, clench and unclench their fists, wiggle their fingers, etc. (as happens after relaxation at the end of a yoga, Pilates or aerobics class) goes some way to prepare the student for leaving the studio, but not really for getting up and working on movement! Yet deep relaxation is key to working on movement at the start of a session.

The Key to Body Space

When I was doing my Decroux training in a cold, damp, underground studio in Paris, we would begin each class with a five-minute jog. The idea was to 'get us going'. The body was made to move without prior stretching, to warm us up for the subsequent demands the technique would make on our bodies. We geared ourselves up for this—sort of 'grin and bear it' type thing—dodging the other 'grin and bear it' bodies in the small space. Of course, when the body is driven in this way, it operates in a state of tension as it has to steel itself to work. The body has moved from the business of getting to class—i.e. tubes, bikes, traffic, rain, stress, thoughts unconnected with the coming class—straight into immediate busy-ness. Well, why not? It is good to leave troubles outside the door of the studio, but it isn't quite so good to go for the 'mind over matter' thing—in fact, it is ultimately unhelpful where movement training is concerned. 'Mind over matter' suggests a blocking out of matter. Some people talk about stiff upper lips, etc. Yet this creates a very real problem that is physical: the body pushed into movement first thing in this way has been denied space in which to define itself, and a body denied space has difficulty doing precisely the things we ask an actor to do—i.e. fill the space. How can a body fill the space when it has been given neither boundaries nor room to feel its own internal space?

To explain this better, let me give you an example. In my second year of Decroux training I secretly fitted in training with Monika Pagneux and Philippe Gaulier. I say 'secretly', because training in two places was, quite rightly, frowned upon. Monika would start the class with the blessed words '*Prenez un tapis et un tube…*' ('Take a mat and a tube…'—a cardboard carpet roll, in this case.) We put down our mats and placed the tube under the length of our spines on the mat. Sometimes there were yelps of discomfort as the hard tube put pressure on sensitive spots, but gradually the class became quiet. The mat gave us a boundary—a quiet space to concentrate on our bodies; a chance to listen to our body, feel the bones and muscles and how they were conjoined; giving the body a space to feel and be felt. No mind over matter here—rather mind *into* matter—the essence of acting, if you think about it. After five minutes or so we removed the tube, still lying flat on our backs on the mat. Bliss! The tube, by pushing the vertebrae out of their accustomed position and supporting them, had released the muscles on either side of the spine. This had allowed these muscles to relax, which meant that, after removing the tube, the back lay on the floor like a baby's. You could feel the shoulder blades, the space between them; vertebrae and space between them: the sublime organisation of the internal structures.

The more physically demanding the work, the more useful deep relaxation can be at the beginning of class. Deep relaxation is not something I would advise in a first-term or a one-off session. The students need to know and trust each other and their teacher.

Relaxation creates space; space allows the body to regroup and it allows the mind into the body, making for an efficient partnership. There is no imposition of technique, rather an invitation to discover how a body is held together efficiently so there can be an intelligent physical response to the subsequent learning of technique.

Deep relaxation inevitably means sleepiness and grogginess afterwards, but these can be swiftly and safely remedied. Very deep relaxation I do in pairs:

Groggy Space

One of the pair (A) is to relax, and their partner (B) is to aid that process, whether it be to assist (as in 'assisted breathing'), gentle manipulation, or simply holding. At the end of the period of relaxation, B helps A to stand. A keeps his or her eyes closed throughout. B leads A about the room very slowly, careful not to let them bump or even brush against anything. As A becomes a little more comfortable in this, then B might go a little faster, and just use the pressure of a hand on the small of A's back to guide him or her. This might take five to seven minutes. Then the pair stop, A's eyes still closed, for at least a minute. The other senses of touch, smell, hearing and feeling have all been sharpened in this simplest of actions. All the As are now wide awake: mind in matter.

Local Relaxation

Local relaxation—i.e. the relaxation of a specific part of the body—can be very helpful prior to a particular physical exercise.

There is a breathing technique I have devised following my own surgery in 2000. The surgery played havoc with the pectoral muscles on the right side of my chest. My right arm, as a result, was very tight, unable to lie comfortably on the floor behind my head and the elbow unable to reach higher than the head. I perfected what I call 'steam-breathing'.

A child breathes onto the window pane on a cold and foggy day. A little patch steams up, and the child happily writes their name or draws a little picture on the glass. We've all done it. In steaming up the window, a particular kind of out-breath is employed: no blowing out of the air, but a very soft, soundless breath with the mouth open and the jaw totally relaxed. Now we apply this breath:

Steam-breathing

Sit comfortably on the floor or on a chair with your eyes shut. Very slowly raise the right arm out in front of you until it reaches shoulder level. See how slowly you can do this. Notice the weight of the arm itself. Notice the slower you go, how exhausting it is. Now relax. Next, place the fingers of the left hand into the right armpit. The palm of the hand lies just above the right breast over the pectoral muscles. Place the right hand on top of the left. Now breathe into the area under your hands. You should gradually feel the area expand on the inhalation. On the out-breath use 'steam-breath': have the sense that you are steaming up the area under your hand with this very soft out-breath. Repeat seven or eight times. Now pause, and then lift the right arm very, very slowly. Notice the difference. It is remarkable how much tension we carry in the pectoral muscles. Mothers constantly picking up their babies and toddlers often sustain painful arms and hands to the extent that it is sometimes difficult to pick up even a cup of tea. The problem is not tired arms—it is tense pectoral muscles.

Steam-breathing allowed me to regain full movement in my right arm by the end of three weeks, instead of the three months I was told it would take. Steam-breathing can be used in any part of the body.

So, relaxation is not about lying on a sofa with a G&T in front of the telly. That is comfy diversion.

Total relaxation of the muscles occurs only in death—so we don't want that. We want relax-actions: actions that allow the muscles to relax, realign and regroup in a space where the mind can observe what is happening. In this way, the body is given the time and space to be recognised. It becomes a partner.

Chapter Four

Getting the Best Out of Technique

The Role of Alexander and Feldenkrais Methods

During my own training, when I got up to improvise, I began to have a horror of my left arm: whatever the subject of the impro, my left arm would bend at the elbow and my fingers would come to my chin in a pensive sort of way. I couldn't stop it. It happened every impro, often, tediously and maddeningly. Years later I am very aware of the 'arm syndrome' when working with acting students in impro: movements of habit that the actors cannot seem to escape from—perhaps don't want to move on from. These movements have often been reinforced or created out of the techniques studied; the very techniques providing the crucial building blocks have literally blocked the actor in to the extent that an improvisation (like my own back then) may, paradoxically, become predictable.

Of course technique is essential, but the way our souls and bodies usefully absorb that technique is a very individual thing, and this is where both the Alexander and Feldenkrais Methods are so useful. You will find the Alexander Technique taught in most drama schools now, and sometimes the Feldenkrais Method. The latter (which finally put a stop to my arm thing) is a fascinating and thoroughly enjoyable co-essential to the rest of my work.

If you ask someone to sit up straight, they will often do something rather peculiar that makes them look as though they have swallowed a broom handle. Here's an alternative:

The Pendulum (Seated)

Sit on a chair, comfortable, with a sense that you are sitting up straight. Now imagine someone has told you to sit in this position for a two-hour lecture. You might notice that your muscles will contract, you immediately feel a pain in your neck or your knee— it is a pretty ghastly thing to imagine. Now close your eyes and gently sway the body from right to left, the base of your spine through to ten inches above the head moving as one pendulum—small movements back and forth. Now take the movement forwards and backwards and then round in a small circle. All movements are very slow, and see them in the mind's eye whilst doing the exercise.

After a few minutes, stop, open your eyes and notice: you will feel something, however small, has changed. The neck might feel less tense, the body a little more comfortable, the idea of the two-hour lecture may not seem such a nightmare. There will be a difference. Once you begin to notice a change, however small, and feel what is happening in the body, then you are on a road called 'freedom through discovery', because you are just beginning to discover another way the body can work.

This exercise is ATM (Awareness Through Movement), the Feldenkrais Method, designed to make us aware of how we have literally learned to learn; how 'free' movement as we perceive it is often constrained by our habits or habits that have unwittingly been imposed on us. Both the Alexander Technique and Feldenkrais Method are not about learning a new technique, but about how we *approach* learning itself. They are about unlearning movement patterns that are not useful to the efficient and creative functioning of the body. Though separate practices, they both have 'noticing' at their core. ATM classes tend to involve numbers of small movement sequences guided verbally by a practitioner. In an Alexander lesson, a practitioner will often use their hands to guide a student and aid their kinaesthetic awareness. Both techniques work with individuals and small groups.

The results of both, it would be fair to say, are more efficient breathing, a sense of connection between the body parts, an understanding of pain, but most importantly a stronger sense of 'self', with the freedom to move in unexpected new ways with ease and efficiency. The body becomes a means of discovery. It has the means now to *use* technique rather than be imprisoned by it. It can improvise...

However, I would say, and I know my Feldenkrais and Alexander Technique colleagues would agree, these Methods work fantastically well with other movement techniques and are not a replacement for them. Actors can all too easily get into a 'method' to the extent that that method can be apparent in their acting. I've seen performances where *all* the actors are tremendously good at sitting on the floor in a particular way with terrifically straight backs. It is not the purpose of either Method to be visible in this way. An actor must never parade their training onstage.

As teachers, it is very easy and often appropriate for us to talk about the 'right' way of doing things. Students like nothing better than to find the 'right way' to move, use the voice, enter the stage, play a role... 'Which is the right way to breathe in this exercise?' is an often-asked question. We all want certainty and security, but 'right' for the actor is a dangerous word as it limits investigation and consequently the actor's freedom. The wonderful thing about the Alexander and Feldenkrais Methods is that they don't ask you to ask, 'What is right?'; but they ask you, 'What can happen?'

Lecoq's Seven States of Tension

Jacques Lecoq taught his students an exercise involving seven different states of tension. Collaborating with an actor who had been an ex-student of his, I learned her version of it. We would use it as a warm-up, as a way of exploring character and as a springboard for improvisation.

The exercise explored seven physical states of being, beginning with a state of relatively low tension, laid back, floppy, drunken, and finishing at number seven, in a near paralysis of tension where movement was almost impossible, in a state you might associate with extreme trauma.

I became very interested in the Seven States, especially how they progressed one to the next, and began to work on them with my own acting students. Each state had its own character, and each state could experience all the other states—in a flash, or over the course of a whole play. To make it a really useful tool for the actors, there had to be a living connection between the states that was first internalised, and then played with. Otherwise the exercise would never become a tool, but just be 'something we did as a matter of course in the second year', over and finished, superficial. At LAMDA I began to develop the exercise until it became a process that took a term to complete, with performances devised by the students. What fascinated me was how the process of the exercise was an extreme version of *The Pendulum* exercise I described in Chapter One: the actor having to move beyond his or her accustomed range in order to re-find that range, or, in T.S. Eliot's words, so pertinent for actors:

> ...to arrive where we started,
> And know the place for the first time.

First, there is the question, 'Why seven?' There could, of course, be any number of states of tension. How many states does a rope go through in becoming taut? Just the business of waking up would involve any number of states of tension before the subject could focus on anything in particular. These particular seven states are useful, because seven happens to be a useful and efficient number in this exercise.

*

I have already intimated that each state is associated with a physical way of being, that has its own dynamic, its own centre and its own character—depending on who is doing the exercise. The actor learns the states in order, one to seven, so that there is a natural progression from one state to the next. Each state has its own peculiar rhythm, time, space, movement and emotion depending on the actor's play (and by 'actor' we are talking here about an already-centred actor).

State One is the foundation stone of the other states. If not enough time is given to this state, the actor will not find sufficient depth in the other states and will waste his or her time. At the end of State Seven, I ask the actors to return to the first state.

After establishing 'Why seven?', there is then the question 'Why tension?' Of course, there is tension in everything, and between everything. Nowhere is this truer than on the stage where even the positioning of a chair can affect the tension levels of a scene, as we saw in the previous chapter. By 'tension' I do not mean 'tenseness', and it is important to distinguish these two words. I do not mean the tenseness one associates with nerves and stress (though this does come into play in the exercise). I mean the tension at which activity is carried out—the tension behind activity, and therefore in activity. Where the Seven States are concerned, it is the tension that evolves from each state, and feeds the next. Locating the centre of each state, the centre of the tension, is most of the work. When this is achieved, then the actor can play from that centre without losing his or her own.

State One

Rather than see this as the 'relaxed' or 'drunken' state, I developed State One into the state of self-containment. The state of non-interference. The state of total connection of the self to itself, unaffected by any outside influence. For the student actor it is the hardest state to master, and requires the most time.

It is a state of total calm, but also of total movement. Imagine a large seaplant growing on the floor of the ocean where it is deepest and where it is at its most still. The plant seems immobile, but if you observe carefully there is perpetual movement. Supported by the water around it, the tiniest movement in the water, resonance of a ripple miles away or miles above, causes a tiny movement in a leaf, and now no part of the plant is unaffected, because all parts are centrally connected and supported.

The movement is felt throughout the organism. It has no punctuation, no dynamic rhythm: it is pure flow at its subtlest. 'Like an embryo in a sack of fluid?' Yes, in terms of the fluid, but no, in terms of the movement: the embryo stops, flips and turns, tadpole-like. There is staccato in the developing young. There is no such jerkiness here: it is the starfish alone in the deep; the jellyfish in the still shallows. The movement comes from the centre, the hara, the belly, and in the actor that means two inches below the navel. The movement comes from here and moves outwards, but also passes through here from the outside. 'Here' is the connecting junction.

The actor in State One: The actor sits on the floor in the most comfortable position possible and imagines they are in a bubble of liquid. The fluid in the bubble surrounds and supports them. It is above and below; they are right in the centre of their bubble. Nothing can penetrate this bubble:

there is, as I said, no interference. The actor must take time, possibly up to ten minutes, just to feel the bubble and get a sense of it without doing anything. There is always a desire to 'do': to move, scratch and reposition. The actor becomes very aware of the difficulty of total stillness prior to action.

The tiniest movement in the little finger will displace the fluid and consequently affect the rest of the body: there will be a resonance throughout the body, passing through the belly and connecting to the other limbs. Resonance does not mean reaction, and the actor needs to feel how that tiny finger movement might very slightly open the hand a degree, and then travel down the arm—only perceptible in a tiny rotation or lift of the elbow, and then on—the rest of the body not waiting to be affected, but simultaneously resonating to this movement. The legs are all-important here and are not just to be sat upon (thereby getting cramp!). Even if they do not demonstrably 'move', movement must be 'felt' in them as a result of the tiny finger movement. They are alive, connected starfish-like to the centre. This 'feeling' in the legs prevents stiffness, keeping the whole body alive with the possibility of movement.

I ask the actors to be aware of the spaces between the fingers and the toes, under the arms and between the shoulder blades. State One is neither a floppy state nor a swimming state. There is no need to move, no will: movement is just something that happens as a result of the delicate balance between the limbs. 'Oh, like a spaceman!' No, because a spaceman is exploring and the movement is wafty. This is not a wafty state! At a constant tempo, the movement is very subtle and graceful; sometimes it is a state of perpetual awkward grace. It is also a very vulnerable state, for, though there is safety in the bubble, this state of being has no system of defence of any kind, nor any social terms of reference. How to give an example of that quality of movement? Older actors sometimes remember the way the strange globules of pink and green travelled across cinema screens prior to the showing. That had something of State One's quality of movement. Screensavers also have something of it in their 'abstract' setting, but by and large go too fast and have no apparent centre.

It takes a great deal of time to master this quality of movement, and one can look at it as an exercise in extreme refinement of articulation. To watch, there is an apparent lack of tension, yet it is the tension of a complex mobile, connecting and affecting each of its parts.

In State One, none of the actors' limbs reach full extension: there is no need to reach out, only to move and be moved in the bubble. A tiny movement in one direction is balanced by tiny movements elsewhere. There is no need to reach out as there is an absence of will in this blissful state of containment. It is precisely this containment of speed, quality and dynamic that make the state so difficult for the actor.

Continuing State One: The actor has been sitting for possibly twenty minutes in their 'bubble'. Can they, without compromising the quality of movement they have found, come up to stand in the bubble? If they constantly maintain the image of the bubble and their place in it, surrounded and supported by water, especially from below, and if they have really 'felt' the movement travel their entire body and not allowed the legs to turn into a sitting platform, then yes, this is possible and will be a natural continuation of the movement. To watch, there seems to be virtually no 'tension' as we understand it in this state. For the actor it is a state of total living tension.

State Two

Comfortable in the bubble, the actor sits, stands, utterly self-sufficient in their awkward grace. When the actors have fully mastered this quality of movement, I ask them to begin to sense something beyond the bubble (later, I have no need for these instructions, as the actors find their own time to move on), something they might eventually reach out to… The reaching arm finally extends just that bit further, the eyes are searching to lock on to something, shadows beyond the bubble begin to have definition, there is a consciousness of things outside, developing… the reaching continues, and the bubble bursts. We are in State Two.

The fluid in the bubble is gone and the actor lands. There is the state of connection with the ground. The actor is earthed. French aeroplanes prepare for '*atterrissage*', a coming down to earth—a good word for 'landing'. I ask the actors to drop their centres right down into their bottom, their balls, or their perineum. Paradoxically, as the actor is earthed, the space becomes huge. I ask the actors to look up at the vastness of the sky, and, because they are earthed, they are comfortable with it, at home with it. They have perspective. The actor, in landing, now has weight and their body reflects that weight as well as the space around them. This is not a person to put behind a computer in a tight suit. This person has a natural and consistent rhythm: a manual rhythm apparent in work and in rest. This, in part, is the noble savage, Hiawatha, Seth from *Cold Comfort Farm*, Corin from *As You Like It*… Mrs Proctor in *The Crucible*… even the late Betty Tucker from *The Archers*! Unhurried, solid, able to be still and watch, but with a certain 'Adam Bede' innocence; people who can gaze over the land and be utterly present, but conscious of their place in the roll of generations. Practical people, good with their hands. Their pace is measured, unhurried, and there is self-assurance in each step. It can be very sexy as well, but with no provocation. It is a very beautiful and satisfying state to work on. It can also be considered the 'cool' state.

Tools for actors in State Two: Bringing the centre down in order for the actor to 'land' can be difficult, and many actors tend to confuse weight with heaviness in this state. I use a number of exercises to bring the centre down including *Flipper Feet, Bums to the Sky* (see Appendix), and:

The Feldenkrais Leg-drop

1. Lie on your back with your knees drawn up and your feet planted on the floor, the width of your hips apart.

2. Pull the trouser on your left thigh towards you to pull the foot off the floor.

3. Let go of the trouser and let your foot fall back to the floor. Notice the noise it makes, the feel of the fall. Try it on the right and compare.

4. Both feet on the floor, make circular movements with the ball of the left foot on the floor where it lies, pushing hard into the ground. Now increase the movement, so you work all round the foot, pushing your toes, then the outside of your foot, then your heel, then your instep, into the floor in slow circular movements. Now rock the foot between heel and toe.

5. Rest. Now lift the trouser of the left thigh again, pulling the foot off the floor. Let it drop as before and notice the quality of the sound on the floor and compare it with the right foot.

6. Come up to stand very slowly and take a walk. Compare right and left feet.

7. Repeat the process with your right leg.

The more the actors can feel their centres lowering, and their weight on the floor, the more they can feel the space around and above them. I tell them to gaze into a vast landscape and feel its size inhabiting their bodies and reflected in their eyes. Perhaps a state of wisdom as opposed to intelligence.

Improvisation in State Two: Give the actor a table and chair, a knife and fork and preferably a plate of real food. Look at the business of eating in this state: the weight of the forearms on the table, the concentration on the food, the silence. The way of eating the bread with the fingers—no fancy stuff here, but equally there is no uncouthness. The hands holding the knife and fork are used to tilling the land or being in the land. (It's unwise to see this as a sort of peasant-only state, because the state is to do with a level of tension so cannot be pushed into a social pigeonhole.)

Now put a telephone on the table as well. The actor has to make a phone call, at some point. It's a fairly fiddly piece of machinery for a person in State Two. Look for the vocabulary of the state when faced with this mechanism: the potential loss of dignity for the person who is used to dealing with people face to face, on the land. A tricky thing. State Two has its grandeur, its gravitas and its inevitable vulnerability.

I keep the actors in State Two for several sessions and then I let them walk, and walk, and walk.

> 'Feel the centre gently begin to move up. Take your time and keep walking. It rests at about one inch above the navel. Keep walking, we are moving into State Three, the neutral state.'

State Three

Neutral is neither monotone nor bland. It is a state of being that is absolutely present: no future, no past, no baggage, but total awareness. The state of being extraordinarily ordinary. It is a state of centred tension; the cat sitting peacefully on the wall is ready, in its peacefulness, to leap up the tree should a victim bird present itself. State Three is not a state to be in for long. Humanity forbids it!

The Walk

(See also 'Centring Exercises' in the Appendix.)

1. Walk around the room.

2. Gradually engage the balls of your feet so you are rolling through the feet to the toes.

3. Use the balls of your feet as springboards, push-off points.

4. Notice any change in your eyes and your focus.

5. Keep pushing off the balls of your feet until you spontaneously break into a little trot. Keep pushing off until you are leaping across the room.

6. Now walk engaging the heels only. Notice what happens in your sternum and your eyes.

7. Return to pushing off from the balls of the feet. Notice the tiny lift in your sternum. Alternate heel walk with 'push-off' walk.

8. Return to your 'normal' walk. What has happened? By going to extremes you will have re-found your true centre and everyone will be walking at the same speed: clear, ready, no baggage.

State Four

Keep walking and let a little hesitation into the walk. A grain of uncertainty. You become a little less alert, and a little more wired. The centre rises to the upper sternum, about three and a half inches below the base of the neck. The sense of being grounded is receding or is being actively discarded. As a result of this, the actor finds it hard to stay in one place, physically or mentally. The body is in the state of continual distraction, a sort of friendly hyperactivity. I say 'friendly', because the actor may be somewhat bothered by their inability to remain focused, but is not unduly upset. Indecision and wonder characterise this state, with a certain amount of absent-mindedness. Monsieur Hulot! A conversation with someone in State Four might go something like this:

X: Hello Christopher! Don't often see you in this part of town.

State Four: Oh, hello... um...

X: Malcolm.

State Four: Malcolm, of course, how lovely. Goodness! Did you see that car? It's just gone past... Now that reminds me... John?

X: Malcolm.

State Four: Malcolm. Well, Malcolm. There's a nice little café over there. Shall we? No, I better not, I need to go to... now where was it?

X: Well, another time.

State Four: Dammit, John, let's have one now. It's been ages. Look, doesn't that person over there remind you of Old Dobbs?

X: Old Dobbs?

State Four: I hope I don't get a parking ticket. Oh, never mind. Here we are, John.

X: Malcolm.

State Four: Who's Malcolm? Gosh, it's raining. Do you want an umbrella? I always bring two. At least I thought... (*etc.*)

And so it goes on and on and on, but always with plenty of gentle energy. The feet are light, if awkward. They don't like stillness. We have all experienced this state. Usually when there is a little bit too much going on and there are too many choices on offer, too many decisions to make. Laughter and tears come easily in this state, but they pass easily too.

I get the actors to play with degrees of this state: feeling the state's centre, its connection with the throat, mouth and cheeks (be careful to keep the mouth open to remove unnecessary tension from the jaw) can be enough to make one feel unsure, to look around, to become curious. When the actors really get into playing this state there is suddenly so much to be distracted by, so much uncertainty, that the state has to change. One might expect breakdown, but the body is not unduly stressed as yet. I ask the actors to move the centre up again.

State Five

State Five's centre is a hard bullet that lies between the eyes. It is from here the character operates. It is a state cut off from heart and lungs. Peripheral vision is limited as the state lacks the expansion afforded by the out-breath. The centre is hard, the body is hard: it acts in one way and cannot compromise. It moves in certainty. In this state, things are either black or white. He is never wrong. His world is about fulfilling his purpose. He has authority, but is not 'an authority'. 'Unyielding', 'determined', 'having tunnel-vision' can all describe this state. A mild version of this 'bullet between the eyes' state is the fierce school ma'am or Mr Bumble the beadle from *Oliver Twist*, or plenty of politicians… In its more extreme form, it is the fanatic and fundamentalist.

The actors move about, becoming more didactic and intolerable by the second. In a group, one realises this state is close to madness. I now ask the actors to imagine that their centre, the bullet between the eyes, is growing in size and heating up. All tension in the body is concentrated between the eyes. The bullet is a bomb waiting to go off.

State Six

It goes off! The tension has exploded out of the body. It is now outside the body—but this is not a release, because the body is centre-less, it has no anchor. It now rushes towards this exterior tension to find some sort of stability. This is not possible, hence hysteria and euphoria. The character cannot ground. We are in the world of melodrama, grand opera, crisis. There is no balance, only extremes. The tiniest joke is hysterical, the smallest mishap a tragedy of terrific proportions. Leaps of ecstasy, crashes of despair.

We work on playing and overplaying the melodrama of some of the earliest silent movies: all is gesture—huge gesture. Yet if we were to remove the limbs from the body in these extravagant movements, the torso would show no toil, no strain, it would be empty of tension, of power, of centre. It is an emotional body only in that emotion exists outside of it.

This is a fun state to work in. I get the actors to work on lightness and bigness before improvising. Then, in pairs, they improvise tiny, banal scenes: 'The gas bill has arrived.' 'The gas bill is less than I expected.' 'The gas bill hasn't arrived!' All this is improvised in grand opera: a huge voice supported by a huge, gesturing body (and very centred as far as the actor is concerned)—but no apparent internal tension. Crisis and euphoria only.

State Seven

Where can this state go? We long for stillness, but stillness cannot come from an uncentered melodrama. In the end, there is implosion replacing explosion: the inability to find a centre blocks the body, and this is State Seven. There is now physical breakdown following the hysteria. The character simply cannot explode any more but wants to. The body blocks and becomes solid tension. It is hypertension of such a degree that the muscles actually oppose movement. To move an arm forward a few inches requires one hundred per cent from the muscles, and is a monumental task. Where is the centre now? It is impossible to tell. When there is total block, there is no functioning centre, no source of energy and connection.

This is the most physically taxing of all the states for the actors, and though I use the term 'implosion', for the actor the process is the absolute opposite of muscular implosion. The actor needs to feel the muscles breathing or they will suffocate. They need to be an efficient and vocal actor in this state. We prepare with a simple exercise:

Wrestling

Tenseness is 'gritting your teeth and bearing it'. Tension, on the other hand, allows things to expand, it breathes. In this exercise, as a pair, go for each other's legs, locking on to the legs with your arms. The idea is to get your partner to the floor. Evenly matched partners will reach a point of stability through tension: all the muscles working outwards in the act of wrestling. Like this, the body retains space and can breathe—sing, even! But the effort is enormous.

Working against someone else in this way allows you to feel this muscular expansion. When in State Seven, your 'partner' is the surrounding space. Your own body fights against this. The state is about implosion and block, but you must work outwards to convey its desperate nature. Working seriously on this state will lend gravitas because you can only play extreme block when you are fully anchored yourself.

The boiling point of State Seven cannot continue indefinitely: it is far too great an expense of energy. The state has to finally give way and return the body to its original matrix. It has to regenerate. I ask the actors to pause; the body frozen in its tussle with space does not change its form, but the muscles start to release and soften. There is something melancholic in this process of giving up the fight, of yielding.

'Where next?' I ask the group, but they have gone on ahead. They know, and silently return to the bubble. Their movements are utterly connected, free from obvious tension, but all in quiet suspension; private, safe, self-sufficient. State One was the hardest to master, but now there are none of the jagged edges some of the actors found difficult to avoid previously, none of that jerky rhythm and awkward fidgeting. Battering through from States One to Seven, they had spontaneously re-arrived at State One and 'known the place for the first time'.

The Seven States are a journey for the actor and for the actor's character, the former playing with the changes of centre, the latter living them. The states are reference points occupying a particular place in a particular scale. As an experience within training that can be repeated in many different ways and situations, it is very powerful and pushes an actor hard to feel stillness and block and all between, through movement and tension.

Playing with the Seven States of Tension

Taking Half an Hour

Half the group move through all the states, from One to Seven and back to One, really taking time to feel when one state can, and then must, move on to the next. With a full half-hour this demands a great deal from the actors as it requires extraordinary concentration, awareness and physical energy. I always insist the actors return to State One after Seven as it revitalises them as well as being, in part, the point of the exercise!

Seven States Across the Floor

The actors travel on the floor. They cross the studio (you need a large studio for this) passing from State One to Seven and back to One. On the floor they are picked up by each other's rhythm and are carried by it. It is the calm, the storm, the calm.

On a Chair

Eyes closed. Over seven minutes, very small. I give the actors one word, very general—for example, 'hope' or 'grief'—and, remaining on their chairs, they travel through the states in concentrate. I always give them music (nothing with too much of an obvious rhythm) and sometimes a prop: a briefcase on the lap, a book or small article of costume. The states become charged with emotion. A person's dark night of the soul.

Improvisation

Think of a mundane situation that can encompass States One to Seven. As an example:

You are driving to the supermarket listening to a very beautiful piece of music on the radio. You are fine, comfortable in the bubble of your car, enclosed in this delicious music. Connected and at ease. State One.

You park the car in the multi-storey and set off to the shop. The place is huge, but you are used to it, knowing exactly where you are going. The space does not overwhelm you, in fact you feel quite gung-ho about the whole thing. State Two.

You finish shopping and make your way out. Very present. No rush, no regret. State Three.

You put your hand in your pocket and freeze. No car keys. You are distracted: 'Where did I put them? Did I have them at the checkout? Drop them somewhere? Did I ever have them?' State Four.

Suddenly you remember you always hide them on top of your front right wheel—even though you've been told time and again this is a bad idea. How stupid you have been, and let's not waste any more time. State Five.

You march into the car park, reach your parking spot and the car is not there. Stolen! You rush hither and thither—calling anyone you can see for help. Everyone comes running. You are beside yourself, literally. State Six.

You turn your head. Your car is in the slot behind you, and you have been looking in the wrong space. You can't even explain. The mortification, exhaustion and hopelessness of the last ten minutes clogs your arteries. Tenseness invades the body. State Seven.

Until the actors go through these banal scenarios they fail to see how they can return to State One—or, rather, where State One now takes them (from this example, I don't know!).

Creation of Pieces

I give each actor two weeks to prepare a three-minute movement play (no words) encompassing States One to Seven to One using costume and music if they wish (though I warn them against using songs as this usually tends to overinfluence their work). I help them by giving them a choice of titles, for example:

a. *If Only I Could Turn the Clock Back*
b. *Let Me Remember*
c. *One Foot in the Sky*
d. *Whose is that Doggy in the Window?*

Marlon

Marlon, a passionate, huge and hungry student actor, was known for his hasty and sometimes slapdash style. State One was anathema to him, but by pinning him down, I got him to spend a whole thirty-five minutes in it as a sort of 'kill or cure' policy. What happened was that he did not want to leave it. He saw no reason to reach State Two: to land.

When we started playing with the states and moving through them as a movement exercise, Marlon was not to be rushed. The rest of the group, by some kind of group osmosis, were moving from neutral State Three to State Four when Marlon landed in State Two. There was a sense of triumph in his landing, an unhurriedness and largeness that contrasted strongly with the speedy 'State Fours'. He was revelling in State Two and a beautiful, if harrowing, play began to unfold then and there. State Two opened up huge possibilities for his acting: he hadn't been able to get away from his own physique, his hectic strength; he was used to being typecast into 'crashing bore' roles. Now, in State Two, largeness could be gentle, wise and consequently much stronger. The 'quick to anger' label this Don Camillo wore, could be cast off.

As the rest of the group hurtled into State Five, Marlon was only just moving into the neutral. The noble savage against the backdrop of incomprehensible hustle and bustle. Following the group in this way, at a remove, allowed one to see the relentless progression of the states, how one had to be succeeded by the next—an inscrutable progression with no turning back. The group had returned to State One as Marlon reached the agony of States Six and Seven. It was pure tragedy as one could see so clearly where he had to go in order to find the release of State One!

When the exercise was over, the students remarked how they saw his confidence and openness in his State Two from their standpoint in hectic State Four, and were filled with both compassion and envy, but knew there was no turning back for them either.

Chapter Five

Play and the Importance of Suspension

Suspense is something that universally thrills. Many are the times we cannot put a book down until it is finished, until the dénouement is revealed; we can be on the edge of our seats in a theatre, cinema, at a tennis match. Being 'on the edge' is exciting. Suspense holds us. It is the adrenaline of anticipation—which is why it very nearly kills us!

An audience does not have to be held in a permanent state of excitement, but it does have to be held, and for actors to fully understand this, they must realise the fundamentals of physical suspension.

Often in the second or third meeting with my first-year acting students I have them play *Grandmother's Footsteps*. Each student finds a partner. A finds B. All the As are instructed to sit along the studio wall while the Bs play the game. The As are to watch their partners in minute detail so that when the game is over they can give the Bs a run-down on exactly how they moved, what they did with their hands, eyes, etc., how they appeared to enjoy the game. This run-down or commentary is to last at least a minute.

The game begins. First, to remind you:

Grandmother's Footsteps

One player is Grandmother. 'She' stands at one end of the studio with her back to the others who form a line at the other end, facing her. The 'audience', as I have said, is sitting along the side of the room. The idea is for the players to creep up on Grandmother. She can turn and look at them whenever she likes, and whomsoever she sees moving as she turns is sent back to his starting point to begin again. The person who finally reaches her to touch her, wins, and becomes the next Grandmother.

I love this game and have played it over and over with students, children, soldiers, OAPs, prisoners and doctors. It is universally loved and fun to watch. Why? Because it is all about suspension.

When Grandmother turns round you see something astounding: the players are caught in a wonderful mixture of poses and intricate balances. Their eyes are alive, their focus directed so powerfully at Grandmother that one cannot help being drawn into the game; their bodies are not frozen in time, but caught in suspension, utterly alert. Every fibre of their being is engaged in the game at this moment, just like the moment before a cat springs on its prey. 'What is going to happen?' is our only question, our only thought at this moment.

The poses are worth looking at (if we can call them poses!). Some of my least coordinated, least confident students are holding balances you might see more appropriately in a dance school—and without wobbling. Had the game been an exercise along the lines of 'move about and stop on your left leg when I hit the drum', the chances are that everyone would have fallen over. In *Grandmother's Footsteps*, everyone is a perfect mover.

The game proceeds and the players become more daring. Tactics are employed: a shorter player hides behind a taller one as they both creep up on Grandmother; another begins to leap forward relentlessly and is forever sent back. It becomes a gag. Some players start moving crablike, sideways on, towards Grandmother. Do they suppose she sees less of them this way? Some wear expressions of pure innocence, as though butter wouldn't melt in their mouths, as their feet creep forwards.

There is a lot to look at. After about seven minutes' play I stop the game. As and Bs confer. What did the As notice? They are mostly struck by their partner's tactics and then remember the balances. I ask them whether they noticed their partner's arms, hands and fingers. People do extraordinary things when in suspension: index fingers become like arrows leaving their fellow fingers, hands turn into fists, right and left hands are often telling different stories. What about the head? Did it lead or was it led by the body? Were the eyes boldly up or demurely down? I go on and on questioning, making them notice every inch of their partner's behaviour and physicality in this game.

> 'Did you notice James always stopped on his right foot?'
>
> 'Is that wrong? Has he got a limp?'
>
> 'Of course not! It is something peculiar to James, something to notice, something that is his. James, did you know you did that?'
>
> 'No.'
>
> 'Now you know, you can own it. It'll probably change.'
>
> 'Did the Bs enjoy playing the game?'
>
> 'Oh yes.'
>
> 'But some of their expressions were grim!'
>
> 'Oh yes, but their intention shone through.'

This is it. In *Grandmother's Footsteps*, suspension and intention fuse together. In the player's suspension, his or her intention is understood, and it is the suspension that draws the spectator like a magnet to the intention of the actor. The As scrutinised their partners, but within the context of the game, so whilst studying their partner's physicality they never forgot their partner was trying to win. Suspension allows an actor to 'steal' their audience into the palm of their hand.

When I was training in Paris in the mid-1980s, I had two very dear friends who paid their training fees by doing a very successful street-show up at Montmartre. Every Saturday and Sunday they would compete for space with the other street performers to do their show, weather permitting, five to six times a day. It was gruelling work. One day when they were particularly exhausted, an American fellow-student who was also a successful theatre clown, said to them, 'C'mon, let's make some easy money.' He took my friends down to Place Saint-Germain and perched them on a couple of litter bins. He then told them to point to the sky and hold the suspension. He put a hat at the foot of the bins. My friends pointed upwards, their mouths open—caught in suspension. People walked by and first looked long and hard at where my friends were pointing—i.e. the sky. Then they caught on, laughed or shrugged and dropped a few coins in the hat. They made a lot of money that evening doing a well-known, overused mime gag. But it was all suspension— suspension focusing the audience.

When the body is in suspension, it is light, it is alive. It is a whole-body state, or rather activity, because there is so much movement in apparent stillness. If I ask my students to move around and stop when I click my fingers, it can be a very depressing experience. Stopping can be a shuffling, heavy activity where movement and line die. Decroux said of the geometrical line that a moving actor aspires to: 'The line has the right to commit suicide, but not the right to die.' In essence, the acting situation must not be allowed just to peter out. Suspension keeps the story alive, in the body of the actor.

Pulling Focus

'Who has got the game?' cries the director as the actors are either all pulling focus or hiding away to avoid being noticed.

The director tries again: 'Where should the audience be looking? Whose responsibility is it to direct the audience? Why are we losing interest in what is going on onstage? Oh, yawn, yawn and yawn!'

An actor attempts to draw the focus by leaping forward with a warlike cry. He is stealing the show, thank God. The others don't like it. One in particular, who now tries to pull focus in his own direction. A competition of sorts ensues. The 'play' is unbearable and the director stops it. This is an all-too-often scenario where improvisation is concerned, and no one has written about it better than Keith Johnstone, who, in his book *Impro* (Methuen), gives many wonderful and colourful examples of this kind of apathy and competition when it comes to rescuing a play.

Giving and taking the space appropriately is key to improvisation and indeed to any performance of any kind, and must be addressed right at the start of training. Hence:

'I Throw You the Ball'

This is possibly one of the most valuable exercises for actors at the start of their training, and can be referred to again and again right through the course. It is a game (taught to me by the redoubtable Philippe Gaulier) which I have adapted many times in many situations with actors, non-actors and children alike, and the game is a beautiful reminder to aspiring actors that the business of theatre can never be a solitary one.

There are two very important rules of this game that must be followed:

Rule Number One is that it is your 'favourite game'.

Rule Number Two is that you play it with your 'best friend'.

The importance of these rules becomes apparent as the game takes off. The students are in pairs, and have a ball, usually a tennis ball, between them. The pairs are about ten feet apart. The stages are very simple:

1. Throw (*élan*)
2. Text
3. Point of suspension

In that order only! What does this mean? Player A holds the ball and throws it to Player B. As the ball leaves A's hand, they say (on the *élan* of the throw), 'I throw you the ball', and remain in suspension at the point when the ball leaves his or her hand. Player B catches the ball, holds the suspension on the catch, and in the suspension says, 'Thanks for the ball.' Then Player B returns the ball to A saying, 'I throw you the ball', and so on. Pretty straightforward, but a great deal may be observed in the process.

When the rules are followed exactly then the audience is caught up in the game and directed by the players accordingly. Player A has the ball—the ball is in his or her court, so to speak; they have the stage, they are number one. Then they decide to give the game of 'being number one' to B, who accepts it accordingly (remember it is their favourite game). If A fails to hold the suspension at the end of their *élan*, or speaks before the *élan* and thereby prevents the *élan* from directing the text, then they don't succeed in directing the audience's attention away from themselves to their partner. While A is fiddling about and ignoring the rules, the audience's eyes are with him or her and miss the line 'Thanks for the ball' from B. The audience is confused as to who they should be looking at.

Similarly, B may fail to hold the suspension on the catch. Indeed, it's an interesting exercise to see whether this suspension can be held completely when B says, 'Thanks for the ball', since the desire to accompany the words with a nod of the head is often huge. If this happens, the audience risk losing the game that is between two players. As an exercise in focusing the audience, and giving and taking the space, it is a fabulous device, and one I would recommend to any teacher of almost any subject.

In the early stages of the game, the following tends to happen: sometimes player A breaks their suspension as player B is saying,

'Thanks for the ball.' This returns the focus to A again which is not allowed at this juncture. The game has been given to B, so only when B breaks the suspension may A do the same. The ball is in B's court now.

Some actors get into the throwing and enjoy hurling the ball fast and furiously at their partner, who, inevitably, drops it. The rhythm of the game is thereby lost, and tedium sets in amongst the audience. When this happens I ask the pair if it really is their 'favourite game'. They regroup for a moment and put on fixed smiles like Barbie or the Osmond Family, in order to contrive 'enjoying' the game. This is quite unbearable! Unless the game is done from a place of play, generosity and, above all, complicity, it is dull, dull, dull.

When the basic rules are mastered, I make the game more interesting. Instead of continuing pedantically with 'I throw you the ball', the couple can now make up their own text, but still must stick rigidly to the stages of *élan*, text and point of suspension. For example:

> Player A: (*Throwing the ball/élan.*)
> Text: What's your name?
> (*Suspension.*)

> Player B: (*Catching the ball.*)
> (*Suspension.*)
> Text: Doctor Who.

When the rules are properly adhered to, wonderfully strange dialogues ensue. However, once a player starts to think about their text and the sense (or not) of the dialogue, the rhythm is lost and the audience is lost. Keep the rhythm steady, batting the words back and forth and the audience will enjoy the most bizarre 'conversations'. If an actor becomes stuck in this, it is helpful to make them speak in a pretend gobbledegook language. Then the play of the game and the play of making up a language remove the burden of meaning and as a result much more meaning is made—though it may not be explicit!

As the players become used to the game they can vary the distance between them and regulate the text via the lengths of the *élans* accordingly.

For me, the prime purpose of the '*I Throw You the Ball*' game is to give the space, the control, and the focus to a fellow actor, and for it to be accepted completely, in the moment, and without anticipation.

As time goes on, the players become sensitive to the rhythm and musicality of the ball's movement. To really test this out, I have on occasion removed the balls and placed the actors back to back—but still ten feet apart—sitting down. Now there is no physical *élan* or physical suspension. There is only the idea and feeling of it: the 'seeing' of the ball moving between them. With this variation, this exercise becomes a must for training for radio: keeping the rules, albeit internally, the actors can still have us in the palms of their hands. They do not know what they are going to say, but knowing how to use the space between them, knowing how to 'see' and 'hear' that space, they can mesmerise us just as much.

Bending the Rules

I was once doing a workshop in the sixth form of a boys' public school. The workshop had been loosely labelled 'Drama', and I was very much left to my own devices without a teacher to be seen. There was a twenty-strong group of sixteen- to seventeen-year-old boys and we were to work on the stage of their very nice, newly built theatre. It was a riot. As soon as I was alone with them, the noise level zoomed; boys disappeared and hid in the curtains, cigarettes were lit and I was, basically, an excuse for a good time. It's no good getting angry or upset in these situations. It's quite good just to sit down and give up and then see what happens.

After a bit, we negotiated. I would teach them a theatre exercise and if they could do it we would end the class early. None of them wanted to be there so this was easily agreed. I taught them '*I Throw You the Ball*'. Or course, tennis balls went flying, but I sat quietly. I told them we would watch every couple. After a while we sat down and watched the pairs. Élan, text and the point of suspension were all over the place. They had grasped the purpose, the game, its function very well, but lack of discipline was the saboteur.

Then two boys appeared. They were different from the rest in that they were wearing their school uniform and looked immaculate. Politely, but with infinite cynicism, they said, 'I think it's our turn now,' and amid jeers and cat-calls, they took the stage. Then began the most extraordinary performance: without a glimmer of a smile, yet with a twinkle of complicity in their eyes, they very solemnly played the game adhering meticulously to the rules. For a full twelve minutes they had us enthralled and on our toes as a dialogue ensued that was packed with every expletive under the sun. The barrage of filthy language in which the dialogue was couched was astounding in its variety, but more astounding still was that they got away with it. We, the audience, were silent and still as the game held us in the palm of their hands. Needless to say, the other boys immediately got back to work on their *élan*, text and point of suspension. The class lasted till the end!

A Note on Élan

Élan: for me, this means the 'run-up' in a movement—i.e. what has to be done before an activity is performed. The quality of the high jump is dictated by the quality of the run-up, the *élan*.

Chapter Six

Animal Work

I had been working in movement training and performance for about nine years before I embarked on animal work. My own training had not touched on it at all. It is not a formal part of any training, though is now taught in many drama schools. Animal work tends to result from company exploration and individual actors' observations; or it falls into the category of children's theatre that requires animals for *Alice in Wonderland, Wind in the Willows, 101 Dalmatians,* etc. It can be somewhat whimsical or pantomimy—girls in leotards with funny faces and tails. At least that was my inexpert impression in those days.

My Decroux training, it would be fair to say, focused on honing the body to produce an actor that could express *humanity*: man in his weakness and in his strength, and everything in between. The work was in essence about being human. My shows had been about human beings. At that stage, any transformation work, if you can call it that, was about getting students to enjoy playing a scene in its entirety—i.e. the characters and the furniture, becoming lamps that could switch on and off, the creaking doors of a haunted castle, the TV that winked and buzzed—objects created by the actors through play, timing, slapstick. Creating the cat curled up by the fire would be a gesture at the animal world, fuelled by my enthusiasm and the actors' imaginations. But that was about it.

Over time I became more involved with the work of Théâtre du Mouvement, taking every opportunity I could to follow their research and work with one of their team, Catherine Dubois. Their work on '*animalité*' fascinated me. Studying it closely, I realised that many of the animal movement dynamics, the animal qualities of movement, were pure Decroux—the difference here was the 'otherness', the total loss of body shape, the relationship to the floor, the redistribution of weight. Yves Marc and Claire Heggen, founders of Théâtre du Mouvement, and erstwhile students of Decroux, were informing their research on *animalité* with Decroux principles of movement. It worked. I watched.

In the summer of 1990 I was at the Edinburgh Festival. A South African group called Theatre for Africa was also performing there. These actors were superb: one moment they were rhinos in the bush; the next, motor cars on the highway; then an African chief and his family; next, the bewitching sounds of the veld. They *were* South Africa and they were so by their ability to lose body shape and enter seamlessly into animal, vegetable, mineral, animal… This was no pantomime or gimmick, nothing whimsical here; this was body, heart and soul transformation by very skilled actors.

Teaching at LAMDA, it seemed appropriate to introduce animal work in the second term of the first year. The first term had been spent on the business of 'playing'—reminding the students that acting and playing belong to the same business—now in the second term, it was time to get right inside something. My predecessors had taught 'animal' either by working with masks or creating 'zoos'. The work was very much about observation. Each student would choose an animal to observe and work on in order to 'become' that animal over a period of time. Then from the knowledge gained from 'being' the animal, the actor could choose to inform their character with the essence of a lion or a spider, etc.

Was it enough, I wondered, to observe and practise, practise and observe, in order to get right inside an animal, reach its essence, allow the body to transform into an animal with the ease of a hand slipping into a glove? I thought of my students crossing the studio on hands and knees; the awkwardness of the human body, the bruises, the aching lower backs. Okay, we did this crawling business as babies (most of us), but our limbs were shorter, our knees rounder. I thought of Theatre for Africa, the actors hopping onto high tables as monkeys. They were gymnasts, but they had spent four weeks in the bush following the big game— watching, assimilating, being. They had lived in the same environment as their models, and had derived a particular energy from this. How, as a movement teacher, could I recreate that energy in the studio? How could I facilitate the students' transformation into animal?

I kept thinking of that word *animalité*: animal-ness. What of that *animalité* could the students usefully use *before* they began their animal work—i.e. how could *animalité* itself help their observation of animals?

The dictionary definition of 'animal' is 'a living being endowed with sensational voluntary motion. Animal from *anima*—vital breath.' 'Vital breath'—this had to be my starting point. I would use this vital breath to help the students enter the animal world—a world where the actor must lose body shape. Of course, transformation is the business of the actor, but 'losing body shape' is a better way to describe what happens as a result of animal work. Losing body shape is about reorganising perspective, letting go of a human view of things, and creating a *new* perspective to which the body adapts accordingly.

Before they start work I ask the students to think about a cat. A cat wakes after a long, curled-up sleep; it stretches, yawns, takes a few steps, possibly shaking sleep off a back leg as though dislodging a stray drop of unwelcome water. It then sits very still. Suddenly a dog comes into view. Like a streak of lightning, the cat is up the tree, fur on end, until the dog has gone. Then it comes down for a snack, and then off to sleep again. The process is repeated daily. The actor who becomes the cat does not play out this scenario, but responds to it; responds as the new shape in the environment, a new environment seen from a new perspective—and the beauty here is that the actor, in the work's process, cannot anticipate the animal's response. Consequently, a vast new world opens up to the actor. The cat needed no workout to get up the tree, and though the actor is not an actual cat, by successfully letting go of body shape, and being one hundred per cent in 'catness', they may not actually shimmy up a tree (though it has been done), but they will allow us to believe they are capable of it. Losing body shape has to happen from the inside out, which is why we have to return to the 'vital breath'.

I taught animal work over a whole term. The first two weeks were entirely devoted to breathing: how the anima, the vital breath, can inform the body of its *animalité*.

Breathing

The students start by crawling across the floor on hands and knees. This simple exercise will be the benchmark of their progress. The feedback is varied: 'This hurts my knees', 'This is fun!', 'My lower back is beginning to ache', 'Can we wear kneepads?', 'My neck aches from having to look up…' Normal human comments. Next, in pairs, partners A and B each take turns lying on the floor on their backs. One of the pair watches the gentle rise and fall of their supine partner's thorax. A then slips one hand under the ribs of B's back. The other hand rests just above B's sternum.

The present business is to notice. Where is the movement? Is it in the chest, diaphragm, belly? Is it almost imperceptible? Is there any movement of any kind anywhere else? A slight twitch, for example, in one leg on the out-breath? Just notice. ('Cripes! There's no movement at all! Is he dead?')

Assisted Breathing

As partner A gradually becomes accustomed to the breathing pattern of B, I ask A to very sensitively *assist* that pattern. A gently applies hand pressure: as B breathes in, A will gently press down the upper hand and move it up to an inch closer to the chin whilst the hand under the back 'pulls' the ribs towards the waist, also about an inch. The movement of A's hands *must follow* B's breathing. (If it is simultaneous to the breathing there is a risk of A causing B to hyperventilate.) I call this 'assisted breathing'.

'But this will increase shallow upper-thoracic breathing— everything we are trying to avoid in voice and singing—*and*, anyway, the sternum doesn't rise when you are breathing properly!' This comment usually occurs when B is attempting to make their breathing follow A. However, I reply that in the first place we are working on animal, not voice, but more importantly and more reassuringly, when pressure is applied as in this assisted breathing, B is required to breathe much more deeply so that the breath can eventually be felt in the pelvic area. You have only to reverse the process—i.e. bear down with the upper hand on the in-breath and up at the back—to see that the natural tendency is *not* in that very uncomfortable direction!

The exercise requires great concentration by A. It is easy to lose B's breathing pattern and seductively easy to impose your own. After about seven to ten minutes, the As gently remove their hands. The Bs don't want to move. Some are asleep. 'I feel so much space inside,' 'Every part of me seems to respond to my breath,' 'I had a little cry,' 'I feel high,' 'Every limb is relaxed…' I have only one question at this stage: 'Do you feel more connection between the parts of the body?' 'Of course!' Of course, because when it is possible to feel space, then there is connection. (A child who is hyperactive and has no sense of personal space is unable to connect to what is going on around him or her.) The 'Of course' is unanimous. (One student's chronic asthma disappeared during this work—for good.)

The students swap and the process is then repeated in the sitting position. Partner A now sits, kneels or squats beside B who is sitting cross-legged on the floor. B's position makes it much easier for A to move his or her hands in opposite directions than on the floor. Now B is able to feel how the body may respond in movement to the flow of the breath: the back straightening and lengthening and the chin gently pulling in on the in-breath, and then, on the out-breath, the back curving and folding, and the chin gently tipping back. The Bs begin gradually to increase the movement, and after a while I ask them to continue the movement on the breath without the As' assistance. The movement now increases into the pelvis that tips backwards on the in-breath and forwards on the out-breath (strictly speaking, this is the other way round, but people understand the movement of a pelvis 'forwards' as that found in a pelvic thrust— so the terminology, though incorrect, has stuck. Of course, on a skeleton it would appear to be tipping backwards!)

I now ask the students to return to all fours, eyes closed. 'Keep breathing deeply, and follow the breath with the movement as before.' Now there are no more rules and instructions, only observations. I ask, 'At what point of this breathing/moving cycle is there least weight on the hands and knees?' There is a moment of confusion. 'Hang on! Shouldn't my back be curving upwards on the in-breath—no, I mean downwards...' There are no 'shoulds'.

'Experiment by reversing the breathing/moving patterns. What feels light for one person may not feel light for another.' The point is that when a link has been established between breath and movement, then more links are made: for example, for one student it may be that at the moment when the back is curved as the breath is either entering or leaving the body, they will feel the connection between arms and spine, and legs and spine. The lifted spine allows shoulder blades and pelvis to be drawn upwards, lifting knee and hand with little effort. This is the moment to move. Right arm and left knee lift as a result of the breath and the body moves across the floor in a cross-pattern crawl.

'How are the knees, neck, lower back?'

'Fine.'

Working with the breath like this has revealed to the students their natural capacity to move with ease. The breathing exercises (and there are many more that can be employed) have enabled them to feel the efficient connections between the body parts so the body is now no longer a torso with limbs, but a unit that operates and responds as a whole. Now the students are ready to lose their body shape, because they can feel the shape that they may choose to lose.

I have found it crucial to work long and hard with the breath in this way at the outset of animal work. The students gain enormous energy, and the breathing takes them directly into their physical bodies—deeply relaxing, deeply connecting *and* very safe. 'Connect' is such a buzzword, but it is exactly the right word to use here where breathing and movement are concerned. The students are able, as a result of these exercises, to feel the connections between their body parts, the bones and the different muscle groups, so that gradually they can begin to feel the relationship between one part of the body and another. The muscles are there to do much more than move individual body parts: they are there to adjust, position, and relate one body part with the adjacent body part. They provide a relationship between structure and posture. To 'connect' with our bodies is simply to find a way to allow ourselves to feel the connections that have always existed—though forgotten through abuse or lack of feeling—between every body part. These connections are our inner pathways, where movement is always possible.

Once the actors have discovered the ease with which to move, be it on all fours, rolling, undulating or slithering lizard-fashion in a cross-pattern belly-crawl, then we let the breathing go. The actors return to their normal breathing. Breathing was to discover movement, but to move fast the breathing must be abandoned or else the actors will hyperventilate.

Animal Dynamics

Now I introduce some generic animal dynamics. We look at the animal's relationship to the ground, at what it means to be alert and still, at how it can move across a space at lightning speed... How can, indeed, the body move fluidly from hands and knees to hands and feet? This can be a fun look at evolution speeded up: the kind of pictures you find in science books or at the osteopath's showing the progression from apeman to homo sapiens. Of course, the incentive for the actor to go from hands and knees to hands and feet is speed, but it is also the need for height—the need for the animal to lift its head. I encourage the actors to imagine their eyes positioned on the tops of their heads to allow them to keep their necks supple and parallel to the floor. Now, if they look up, they can feel the lift of the head travelling into the neck, then into the sternum; as a consequence the arms become lighter, reach further forward... Now the toes make contact with the floor. The actor can push forwards and up. The lightness in the sternum means that power is in the legs—in speed and strength. The 'forepaws' can lose contact with the floor, squirrel-fashion. The pelvis has to remain light and supple so that with each step it does not tip from side to side. It is the cornerstone of the body now; from the pelvis the spine can tip down or up. If the spine should curve backwards as the 'animal' comes up to stand, then the pelvis is not engaged and backache will result. Now it is easy to feel the progression from creeping thing to homo sapiens... and the facility in movement that follows is tremendous.

Alert Stillness

A group move on all fours, comfortably. They are a pack. I clap my hands to startle them: alert stillness! That moment when every hair is an antenna. It is not so much a startled response as an '*En garde!*' The stillness of a cat watching a bird before it decides to chase; the stillness of a chicken seeing a cat before it gives the alarm: poised stillness. Now, how to get away?

Fulguration

The extraordinary speed of a running lizard, the cat up the tree, the mouse into its hole. Difficult to describe. 'Fulguration' is good: the movement of lightning that leaves you breathless as to where it came from and where it went. After much floorwork involving rolling, jumping, bouncing, scurrying, crawling and leaping, we go for fulguration.

The game is simple: the pack stops in alert stillness and on a hand-clap from me, they cross a distance of four feet at top speed. How they do it is up to them; be it a roll, dive, etc. My only instruction is to let softness invade the body, then go! The movement happens through softness, not tension, as it has to be for us actors playing at being animals! Gradually, the distance covered is increased until we can make the pack vanish. I feel as though I have been left alone on the veld, overwhelmed by space and silence.

Antennes d'Escargot

Decroux perfected a technique he called '*Antennes d'Escargot*'— the snail's antennae. The name and the movement is pure animal, and he used it to describe a technique that allowed the animal instincts in us to be subtly manifested. The snail's horns are out. You touch one and it does not instantly retreat, rather there is a tiny, instantaneous pulling-back followed by the slow retreat and disappearance of the horn in question. You reach out your hand to touch something, perhaps even to feel an atmosphere; it is as if your eyes are at the ends of your fingers, and before the arm reaches full extension, the 'eyes' sense something. There is a tiny muscular contraction, not a shock, in the biceps, brachialis and triceps; the hand, as a result, is pulled back only an inch, and then the arm gently retreats. It is a subtle business, taking time to locate the muscles and to prevent gasps and sudden movements in the hands. Children love learning this movement and enjoy creating enchanted forests of watery branches by standing one behind the other, their arms moving, very slowly, out in different directions and being eerily forestalled by the *Antennes d'Escargot* technique.

Once the actors have got the hang of this in their arms, we apply the technique to torso, legs, head and the whole body. They work in pairs, moving into each other's space, retreating, approaching, retreating—sniffing each other out, not being sure. The room even begins to smell different.

Research by the Student

Concurrent with this more generic animal work is the students' own research. On the first day of the work I ask the actors to consider an animal they would like to 'do'— make their term's project; make their own. I persuade them to choose an animal they have access to, whether it be in the nearest zoo, at home, in the park, etc. They need time to observe. Videos are good. Sometimes the selection of the animal becomes complicated.

> 'Christian, I've always been told I'm a bit 'ferrety', so should I do something like an elephant?'
>
> 'Do you want to do an elephant?'
>
> 'No, I quite like the idea of doing a penguin.'
>
> 'Then do a penguin'.

Or:

> 'I'd quite like to do an Old English Setter, but my therapist says I must get away from this wanting-to-please thing you associate with dogs.'
>
> 'Do the Setter.'

Or:

'Please can I do a whale?'

'Have you plenty of video footage?'

'There's very little.'

'Then, no.'

LAMDA organises zoo passes, and I ask students to spend as much time as possible observing their animal, getting to know it, getting to know its character.

Into the Animal

We start work on the students' animals from the inside out. The students find a place in the studio where they are comfortable: curled up, lying on the floor, under a blanket, on a chair… Their eyes are to remain closed all the time. I turn off the lights and talk quietly.

'This may take you no time at all, or it may be difficult to concentrate, or you may fall asleep. Just follow the instructions…

'See your animal in your mind's eye some way away from you. Where is it? In a cage, the jungle, the savannah? What time of day or night is it? What is the temperature? What is it sitting or perching on? What is its place? Now zoom in on your animal. Go right inside. Observe the breathing mechanism. Can you assimilate that breathing? Don't try to be logical, but get a sense of its inner atmosphere. Where is its heart? Is there a heart? Look at the quality of the bones, how light, how heavy… The sinews, the muscles, the quality and texture of the blood, the guts. Feel these different qualities inside you. Now slowly move outwards. Notice the quality of the skin… Are there scabs? The texture of the outer layer… Is there fur? If so, is this glossy, mangy, new, old? Look at the claws, nails, teeth, pincers… The breath, the smell of the breath, the moisture in the nose… The shape of the eyes.'

I go on and on. There is no pressure to be the animal, but gradually the internal image expands in the actor's human body, inhabits it, fills it. The breathing and heartbeat is a good starting point as it gives the actor an anchor to come back to. If the animal breathes very fast or has a fast heartbeat, this will inform the actor's body how to adapt to the animal. The panting dog, for example, will inform the human body of a particular kind of movement dynamic. This does not mean the actor will end up breathing like a dog (a sure way to hyperventilation!), but will have the core movement of the panting dog.

At this stage the students quite often want to vocalise—purring, growling, screeching—and this in turn continues to get them inside their animal. Nothing like having to bark to get the breathing to be a whole-body experience!

Sometimes the students drift off or get stuck in the early stages. I simply tell them to go back to step one (visualising the animal), and start again, zooming into its insides. Skipping the stages is like putting underwear on top of outer clothes.

The speed of the work varies from person to person, but I keep them working with their eyes closed over a three-week period. The studio changes—it feels 'other', again, it even smells different. After the first few sessions I ask the actors to choose a place where their animal would like to have a den or a burrow or a perch, etc. I ask them to bring in food, toys, branches, whatever their animal needs. Now they have territory, somewhere to go, hide, be…Their place. Working for so long with closed eyes has sharpened the other senses. They are alert, and there is no space for thoughts such as 'Well, an iguana would never be living next to a penguin, would it?' or 'That owl is disturbing me with its screeching. I'll block it out—I mean, a shark's unlikely to meet an owl…' But that is the beauty of this work: a shark may have to meet an owl.

Opening the eyes is the next step. Each session I have given the students the same tools to get right inside their animal, but now I concentrate more on the eyes: 'Feel the shape of the eye and mould your own eye into that shape.' It is astonishing how the shape of a face can alter when asked to do this. Now: 'Open the eyes.' Looking through the eyes of their animal gets us away from troublesome logic such as 'My chicken has eyes on the sides of its head, so…' which unnecessarily diverts the work.

Now the animals explore. They meet each other. During feedback the students say they don't notice whether A or B is a penguin or mouse, but whether A or B is good news or bad. As a result, some wonderful friendships or extraordinary enmities spring up. I remember a stork and a tortoise that became inseparable, as well as two chimps who had to be constantly separated from fighting each other.

All the while the students are working on their individual animal, we continue to look at generic animal groups—herds, packs, warrens, cubs at play… and birds.

Birds

I devote several sessions to birds. Of all the creatures, we probably use more bird words as adjectives for humans than any other animal: 'duck-footed, crow-like, hawkish, puffed-up, owl-eyed, hen-pecked, strutting, twittering, bird-brained…' The students sit in a circle on the floor. I ask them to close their eyes and picture an English garden at 5 a.m. on a May morning. What do they hear? Slowly, a wonderful soundscape of cooing and twittering emerges. Silence. Now picture a farmyard: ducks, chickens… Silence. Now a rookery.

The three separate atmospheres emerge. I now ask them to repeat the process adding head movements. Now to move. They stand up opening their eyes. A bird's legs bend in the opposite direction from ours. That is not the problem. The problem is to give a sense of bird-walking. We work on feet and balance: the legs lean back, the torso pitches forward. There is pressure in the lumbar region. I ask them to think of flamenco—many dances are reminiscent of courting birds. The sternum is lifted, literally puffed up, the shoulders are down—the weight on the lumbar spine disappears. They can hop, sparrow-like, swagger raven-like, or strut, noticing the natural accompaniment of the head extending forwards and backwards on each step.

But how to fly? It's difficult to do an impression of flying without looking naff. This was a question of concern for me when I was working on the movement for Aristophanes' *Birds*, with director Dictynna Hood, for the Cambridge Greek Play of 1995.

'I need the birds to fly in and out at given signals,' said Dictynna. Well, why not? I remembered sitting in Trafalgar Square just watching the pigeons. They would potter about, so many of them only paying attention to the possibility of scraps from tourists, and then on a mysterious, invisible or even inaudible signal they would take off, in unison. Similarly, coming down, there would be a whoosh—an invasion, and then, once landed, a look of surprise and disorientation—before they got back to the business of pottering about.

I put the actors in groups of five. They were to remain tall, upright, and take small, light steps. They were to cross the rehearsal space very slowly, gradually accelerating en masse until they finished at full tilt. Then the opposite: entering at full tilt en masse and gradually decelerating. It took a lot of practice to feel the force of both acceleration and deceleration within the group, as well as to keep the lightness and the height. We built up the group gradually to include the entire chorus. As they decelerated I asked them to bring in their own bird characteristics, the movements of the head, the neck... They slowed down further, and their bodies reverted to the chicken, sparrow or starling of before. The startled look gave way to a gradual dispersal and pecking about. A clap of hands and they were a startled group, skimming over the stage—heads high—no outspread arms being 'wings', but the dynamic of a flock. The director came in. The flock took off in her direction. 'No wonder Hitchcock's *The Birds* is so scary!'

Animal Experiments

Meanwhile, back at the studio in LAMDA... Was it becoming a zoo, a menagerie, as time passed? I felt self-consciously human amongst beasts ranging from praying mantis to chimp. The smell was different (one student, Daniel, was a dog that actually stank of dogginess), but mostly it was the atmosphere that had changed. The large sunny studio had become claustrophobic. I wanted to open all the windows. Something was tugging at my heartstrings. I looked at the chimp banging his head with a half-eaten banana. Of course, I wanted to set them free.

It was early March, cold and drizzly. In the lunch hour I went and had a chat with the gardeners and park police in Kensington Gardens. Would they mind if I brought three groups of drama students the following morning to occupy a designated space as animals? I didn't go into any detail, save to promise that they would not climb the trees or create any litter. They listened with polite indifference as if I was asking whether I could have a picnic or something.

The next day we all trooped down and each animal, barefoot, found a place to curl up in. The process was to start, as always, eyes closed and still. Their brief was to stay in animal for forty-five minutes. Should the public try to 'interact', I would personally beat up any actor seen to come out of animal to chat. It was wet and muddy. The actors looked a bit miserable and cold. I sat at a little distance, a casual observer.

The animals gradually awoke to their new-found freedom. The transformation was wonderful. The space got inside them, they were at home, they were beautiful. The more I watched them, the more out of place I felt, and the more peculiar and gawky passers-by looked with their prams and accessories. The animals, by contrast, amazed me with their fluidity of movement, their strength, their strangeness. David Attenborough once said he didn't particularly like animals, it was just that he was 'continually amazed by them'. Watching the students, this was how I felt, as well as feeling small and clumsy myself.

People passed by with dogs. The dogs stopped dead in their tracks. Humans weren't supposed to behave like this. The dogs barked, some whimpered pathetically. Their owners tugged at their leads pretending nothing strange was occurring. A little white dog made for the 'hamster' and would not stop sniffing his behind. Some of the bigger dogs trembled, uncertain whether to give chase. Then a huge Alsatian came by, some distance behind his fierce-looking mistress—he was not on a lead. He spotted Chris, one of the chimps, and growled nastily. It had never occurred to me the actors might be in danger from real animals. My concern was interrupted by a lady walking, or rather creeping, towards me through the animals. She had lots of South Kensington carrier bags and looked very excited. She came over to me, breathless with discovery.

'Do you know what's going on? I've only just realised.'

I mumbled something incoherent, my attention on the Alsatian.

'You do realise this is the most advanced form of Tai Chi.' I looked back at her uncertainly as the 'squirrel' seemed to be digging up the grass. Suddenly the Alsatian charged. The 'chimp' snarled and banged the ground nastily. It then began to scream—high-pitched screams. The dog was panic-stricken and turned tail. I held my breath, praying the owner would not suddenly reappear, yet I was so relieved I forgot to worry when the chimp swung triumphantly in the branches of a rather delicate-looking tree.

A party of preschool children passed by, thrilled, identifying correctly each animal. Their carers ushered them by quickly, not looking. One elderly Frenchman patted the wolf kindly on the head and I overheard him saying, 'Now, tell me ze process…' Luckily for him, the wolf only snarled.

I had just begun to relax after the Alsatian encounter, when I saw the park police strolling towards us. Chris, the chimp, was still in his tree, but thankfully the squirrel had stopped digging. Suddenly there was an almighty crash and Dean, our vulture, had landed on the litter bin. I never saw how he got up there. He simply landed and now his head was diving into the bin. Old crisp packets, chip wrappers, Coke cans, banana skins, a whole hideous mess came flying out. The commotion brought Chris down the tree to join in the fun, but a nasty peck from the vulture sent him up a yet more delicate tree. The park police were motionless, watching. I was paralysed with worry—about the animals, the park, my job.

> 'Well, that's a vulture for sure,' remarked one of them. 'Nasty great birds. Now look at that hamster—that's more my kind of animal.'

They moved on.

The hour over, the actors, covered in mud, tramped back to LAMDA grumbling. 'You said we could have forty-five minutes. That was ten minutes at the most.' As in mask work, time had stood still.

Each year I did the park experiment with variations of time and space. One year, to stretch a brilliant—but at the time, lazy—group, I sent in forty four-year-olds from the local primary school to go and play with the animals. These times have been a turning point in the work. The animals have become pretty sure of themselves in the studio by this stage of the term, but outside, they experience space. They didn't have forty days in the veld, but they did taste something, albeit small, of wildness. They were put to the test. After the experiment, the animals appeared bigger, stronger. That hour in the park achieved more than months of physical exercises. The actors gained power through *animalité*—i.e. being entirely 'in animal'—in the presence of animals and humans, and in a present-time that perhaps only animals experience.

Playing with 'Animal'

Two more weeks of term. The students were ready to play. We returned to the floor, curled up, eyes closed… the breathing, the starting point. I asked them to feel the *essence* of their animal, feel it inside, in the fingers and toes, but especially in the eyes. Then I asked them to open their eyes, sit on chairs, but retain this essence. They were humans now with animal essences. They found voices immediately, without thought. The slender loris was French, the hamster Scottish, the tortoise refused to speak, the chimp couldn't stop laughing hysterically.

I interviewed them, chatroom-style. The orangutan, a soulful beast, was now a depressed social worker from Nuneaton who did tango evening classes. The characters that emerged were extraordinary. We played hundreds of situations—railway stations (the sparrow character was a timetable freak literally hopping from one timetable to another), art galleries, waiting rooms, council meetings (the camel character disgusting everyone by spitting gum into the bin at regular intervals), but now the last part of the work was perhaps the hardest and there was only a week left.

Back as animal, moving as animal, but in a human world and inhabiting a human world—as Ratty and Mole with their boat and picnic baskets in *The Wind in the Willows*, or in *Alice in Wonderland*, where the White Rabbit wears a waistcoat, and a sheep knits. The speed at which this can become whimsy—or worse, cutesy—is frightening, hence its place right at the end of a long process. The actor in animal is as in a mask. He or she cannot judge from a human perspective, so cannot decide *how* to play. They just play. Now I was asking the actor to be animal in a world that demanded a kind of human understanding of things, a recognition that a pen is something you write with. We are in the child's world here where the doll's house is frequently filled with toy animals, and the doll mother's brother happens to be an elephant. The child has no problem with these incongruities. With the *animalité* strong, the actors could enter this world too.

One of my favourite improvisations at this stage was to put a chair on top of a table and one chair each side of the table. The scene was a courtroom. The judge sat on the chair on the table and the counsel for the defence and prosecution on each side. The prison was under the table, and the dock a chair apart. I would invite the students to choose roles and take their places to enact the scenes of the trial. The improvisations have been unforgettable. A special treat was Andy's judge. Andy was the hamster, a very good hamster, who ate continuously throughout the proceedings trying to hurry things along. The defence was a very sexy French-speaking tiger, the defendant a small cat of ambiguous innocence, and the prosecution a very frightening wolf. The proceedings reached an impasse so the judge requested evidence and sent the policeman, a tortoise, to get some. He took so long that the judge crept under his chair, curled up, and went to sleep while the tiger made off with the prisoner whom he'd been making eyes at all the while. The wolf shouted so loudly at the policeman, when he finally returned, that he retreated into his shell and wouldn't come out. The judge never woke up...

The final class of term we played the transformation game: a scene was improvised, played in animal. Without warning I would shout, 'Cats', then 'Birds', 'Humans with animal characteristics', 'Dogs'—the scene would change dramatically as the transformations occurred with magical suddenness. The students' bodies were now ready to dive into new shapes like hands into gloves. Losing body shape was an adventure, but now also a skill they had mastered.

The Importance of Animal Work

People love dressing up. Choosing costumes, parading in front of mirrors delights both adults and children. Costuming changes us; the way we stand, the way we move, and even the way we speak. Sadly, in rehearsal, actors rarely get to the costuming bit until the dress rehearsal. Yet their business is to transform; to move from playing Lear, to Oliver Twist, to Mack the Knife, to Gandalf... Transformation is the profession. The beauty of animal work is that it is the costuming of the very guts. Animal work as I have described it is about dressing up with extraordinary attention to detail from the inside out.

Transforming the insides allows the actor to discover what being heavy or light-boned actually entails, what it means to be spineless or indeed spine only. Discovering the essence of Fido, rather than slapping some of his characteristics onto the outside, translates both the actor's mental processes and physicality into something entirely new. It is easy for an actor to discover themselves when deciding how to play a role. It may be an admirable choice, but entering into animal as a rehearsal experiment pushes the body into a playing field the actor could never have imagined. Through animal work, especially over a sustained period of training, the actor gains an entirely *new* perspective, not only on the work in hand and the relationships between the characters, but on the extraordinary possibilities for acting that the body can achieve.

I have used animal work again and again—in preparation for shows, rehearsals of Restoration comedy, Shakespeare, Pinter—to help actors find new body shape. At LAMDA, the students had gone so deeply into the work it was to be a constant resource for what lay ahead, from Greek tragedy to auditions. I have met actors I taught there, well into their careers, who still say, 'When I'm not sure about a role, I just give it to my praying mantis for a bit.' Or 'My antelope got me through my audition with Complicite.' Or 'I never imagined I could jump until I did my frog...' Or simply, 'I still visit the elephant I studied at London Zoo.'

Chapter Seven

Contact Work

When rehearsing a play, suddenly mentioning 'Contact Improvisation' or 'trust exercise' can often have two effects: either the actors sort of go to pieces in giggly heaps of 'Goody, goody, I love all that', or some of the older ones simply walk out. Any form of contact work has to be approached very carefully, and the teacher has to know exactly what he or she is doing and why—and, above all, get involved in a hands-on capacity in order that everyone benefits from the magic of this work.

'Contact Improvisation' as understood in the dance world was developed in the US in the 1960s by Steve Paxton, who called it, 'a conversation on a physical level'. Jan Murray in her book *Dance Now* (Penguin) describes it:

> Contact Improvisers work in pairs, usually having matched themselves as closely as possible in height and weight. They lope round the floor then come together to roll over each other's backs and hips, intertwine limbs, bounce off one another only to collide again with various degrees of force. Partners must trust each other for the spontaneous movement patterns and exchanges of weight develop from wordless communication and confidence that one will support the other.

Mary Fulkerson introduced Contact Improvisation to the UK when she was appointed Head of Dance at Dartington College of Arts in 1973. Apart from it being extraordinary to watch, dancers were excited by the work's ability to provide inspiration in such a therapeutic and healing way.

This book is not about dance, but contact work has a vital place in the training of actors. 'Surely,' I get asked over and over again by people outside the profession, 'the greatness of actors doesn't depend on their ability to roll over each other? I mean, look at Gielgud!' There is always a great deal of misunderstanding when it comes to contact work in the same way as there is about nude models in art schools. There is a feeling of slight embarrassment or naughtiness where intimate body work of any sort is concerned.

My own training didn't do 'contact'. We worked together, performed together, worked our bodies so that we were like fine steel—strong and supple. Many of Decroux's 'figures' we learned solo. In pairs we worked through tension; steel in tension meeting steel in tension. Not so good where human bodies are concerned, so people naturally shied away from contact. Little healing and inspiration here, just the potential for accidents. Would it have been useful to have devoted time to contact? Of course!

The Process of 'Contact'

As social animals we are emotional beings as much affected by those around us as by our internal chemistry. The body is a landscape in the process of constant change, adapting to circumstances in order to be self-regulating as far as possible. We train actors to be aware of this landscape—to explore it and get to know it. We teach what it means to be rooted, to be light, to have weight, how the muscular and skeletal systems function at their best and how our awareness can reach beyond the four walls of a room… But what happens when we are touched?

Now, the pat on the back at the appropriate moment can make our day. The perfunctory peck on the cheek can lead to feelings of abandonment and neglect; a limp handshake can cause physical recoil; being held tight as children by our mothers makes us feel safe and restores our faith in the world. In our somewhat undemonstrative and fearful culture, we have become confused about touch. Touch is for lovers or for fights; it is okay to have pretty explicit bedroom scenes on television, but be careful if you want to comfort a distressed student or a child that is not your own. Touching is not allowed. It is illegal even. You can be accused of 'touching-up'—a perversion of this beautiful word 'touch'. The real purpose of contact work in an actor's training is to look at the process of touch and see the vital role it plays in bringing mind and body together in the understanding and growth of the body's landscape.

What is 'Contact'?

'Contact' is what it says it is: contact between people—physical contact.

I have to 'contact' my students a great deal of the time in terms of adjusting, moving and helping them in their movement. I have to make it clear to them as soon as I begin teaching that I am just as hands-on as an Alexander teacher or any other body-work practitioner. My eyes and ears are not enough in this discipline, I have to be able to feel the body I am dealing with to aid it. (Still, it is important to ask permission before working in this way.) A hand that is trained how to feel another's body does not need to poke or prod, but can tell from simple contact whether a muscle is in tension. It can feel the temperature of a body, it can locate the areas where the subject is 'holding'—where there is a blockage in the flow of energy—where there is lack of vitality, and, indeed, whether a person is ill. An expert hand can feel the internal organs through the layers of skin, fat and muscle. The hand is a sensory organ, but so is the skin which covers the entire body.

The body craves touch—we all know this. Of course the child needs to be cuddled to feel safe and comforted. In the well-known experiment, motherless baby rabbits that were stroked fared better than their unstroked colleagues. Touch is about comfort and grooming, and grooming is about much more than looking clean and tidy.

Carla Hannaford in her revealing book *Smart Moves* (Great Ocean Publishers) looks at the connection between touch and development, citing an experiment carried out in a Canadian elementary school in the early nineties:

> The teachers focused on students that acted up in class and did not do or turn in their homework. Five times a day the teacher would catch these students 'being good', and touch them on the shoulder while saying (in an accepting way), 'I appreciate your doing your work'; when they were acting up, the teachers ignored them. In all cases, within the first two weeks, all the students were behaving in class, and handing in their homework.

But the whole business of touch is a dangerous and confusing minefield. More than ever does the benefit and importance of the right kind of contact need to be re-established. For actors, above all, this is crucial; theirs is the task of portraying the gamut of human conflicts and emotions—in relationship. They need to understand the process of touch.

For example, two characters meet and shake hands. They do not know each other and the gesture is a formality. For a moment, each enters the other's personal space and then returns to his own bubble. Yet something will have changed, however small, through this handshake—something in the play. When a person does not want to shake hands with another, but has to for the sake of form, the pectoral muscles tighten as do the jaw and the pelvic muscles—i.e. the muscles in vulnerable places. The body, quite literally, becomes harder like steel. Now if the actors, or even one of them, unwittingly steels himself to shake hands, then there is a momentary absence of play; an atmosphere is created that might in fact be good for the show, but which the actor is not necessarily aware of. Later on, the same actors, both men, have to hug. The actor who unconsciously steeled himself to shake hands knows intellectually that this is a 'friendly hug'; more, it is the resolution of a conflict: a good warm hug is required. The actor's body steels itself again and the hug is tight and powerful, but no real contact has been made by the actor so the play between them can only advance at an intellectual level.

This may seem pernickety, but an actor's body must become sensible of relationship through touch. Unless the hand, or the arm, or the entire body in fact, is a sensitive, listening, feeling thing that responds and therefore changes on some level, however tiny, acting not only risks being part of an intellectual process (much of which you find in amateur dramatics), but also the actor is denied the wealth of imagination supplied by the body. They are, in fact, limited.

'Contact' in the Drama School

It is important to begin contact work in a very simple way and in a way that the benefits can be seen almost at once.

The teacher of contact must be eagle-eyed. First, I must ask permission of the acting students before doing any hands-on work. This works like a kind of check-in, and gives them a chance to be aware of their own body's needs. Often the body will know instinctively when certain kinds of contact are not okay; being walked over (a crude example), however expertly and sensitively, when the student feels flu coming on, is not a good idea. The body needs to be listened to in many such instances. However, it is easy to confuse manners with tentativeness: 'Are you sure that doesn't hurt?', 'I'm terrified of hurting you—is that really okay?', etc. This kind of dialogue can stop both bodies listening, and engage them in a time-consuming routine:

'No, it's fine'

'Are you sure it's fine?'

'Well, I said so, didn't I?'

'I know, but I'm worried'

'Well, stop worrying… Ouch!'

'Oh God!'

This will totally undermine the process of contact. It is important to start with the simplest of exercises.

Making Contact

Get each student to take a partner by the hand and lead them around the room with their eyes closed.

'What is the nature of that hand hold? Does it feel good, does it provide security in this blind world? We all know a firm, warm handshake is preferable to a limp, cold one. Is the limp, cold hand a result of poor circulation, low blood pressure, fear of contact?'

There is no need to get too psychological here, but rather ask the students to rub their hands, create a charge between them; then rub each other down, groom, wake up the skin.

Waking Up the Skin

Cows

1. In pairs, one of you is a prize cow being groomed for a show. Position yourself on your hands and knees with your neck dropped forward and relaxed. Take deep breaths and slowly 'moo' on the out-breath as deeply and softly as you can.

2. Your partner 'grooms' you: using the palms of the hands, your partner rubs your shoulders, back and buttocks using firm, circular movements. Your partner then goes on to brush your spine gently using the flat of the hand to sweep down the spine to the coccyx. Continue to 'moo'.

3. Your partner moves to your arms and legs: they take your arm just below the armpit, between their hands, and roll the flesh from side to side without taking it off the floor, and then move down to the wrist, rolling continuously.

4. Your partner now places a hand gently on your back. Breathe in gently and on the out-breath sing a note or 'moo' into the area under their hand. When the vibration of the sound is felt under the hand, your partner will move his or her hand to another place. See if you can sing into all parts of your back and buttocks.

'Man, this is new-age!'

No, it isn't. It is work. Leading a person with their eyes closed is an art. The space is quiet. Talking is not allowed. We break and talk about individual experiences of eyes closed-ness: what made Jane feel safe, why Dan had his free hand over his shut eyes as he was being led… was the leading partner really with them, or going too fast, daring them to 'feel safe'? You must on no account let them bump into anyone else. Walking into a lamp-post with eyes open can be traumatic enough. Being led into one with eyes closed can make you, quite rightly, never want to do this work again.

We continue, sometimes up to an hour. Now they are led by gentle pressure: their partner's hand on the small of their back, a hand on the shoulder... until leaders and followers cannot be told apart. As the work proceeds the students with their eyes closed become ninja-like, able to stop, unaided, centimetres from the wall. There is no such thing as 'bumping' any more.

The teacher needs to be cognisant of the group's chemistry. It is hopeless to assume that after two or so years of working together everyone 'ought' to be able to work with each other. Some people simply do not work well with some others. There is no judgement here—it is just a question of chemistry—and it does not help their training to try and force them into uneasy partnerships. Good experiences of this work whilst training prepares them for plenty of uneasy partnerships later on.

In contact, students must choose their partners carefully. Working as sensitively and intimately as this, it is hard to expect them to cold-shoulder any problems they are going through for the sake of the work. The body is at its most vulnerable, and resentment, last night's row, envy or fear will all unconsciously filter into the work and accidents may occur. For this reason I scrutinise the partnering very carefully and sometimes I change it. You can tell pretty quickly if a pair is not totally happy with each other. And if you are about to give them the benefit of the doubt, ask yourself the question, 'Are they working with their chests or their breasts?'

*

'Cover up your chest!' my mother used to yell when we went out into the cold to play. I always liked that word 'chest', as it conjured up buried treasure; chests with nuts and bolts and padlocks lying on the seabed; good workmanship, strong, a strongbox. And that is, in effect, what it is: ribs and a sternum locking in our precious lungs and heart, protecting them in our perfectly crafted personal strongbox. In singing we talk about the 'head voice' and the 'chest voice'. The chest voice occurs when the singer concentrates on the resonance provided by the thoracic cavity. This results in an emphasis on the lower frequencies.

'Cavity', 'box', 'chest'. Notice when you are shocked or startled there is often a quick intake of breath; notice how the chest compresses, the pectoral muscles contract— holding the box together, so to speak, putting another layer over the box. Notice how combative that chest can become in argument, how the box hardens, how the shoulders come forward to protect it. As this box hardens, the energetic connection with the abdomen is cut off, the diaphragm is now redundant where breathing is concerned, and breathing itself is shallow and quick instead of deep and slow. The chest is holding you together—protecting you. The shutters go up, the lid comes down. 'I'm not getting involved' is not necessarily about detachment. In this condition, the chest is not a receptive, listening part of the body—nor should it be. It is fencing: defending your precious organs. There is no talking to fencing.

Breast Versus Chest

As an experiment, I get four actors to walk towards us in an exaggerated, defensive 'chest' mode. They look aggressive, fearful... Their necks disappear, their arms do not swing freely, the easy cross-pattern swing has gone. They are a bit thuggish and have reduced stage presence.

What about working with the breast instead of the chest? The word 'breast' is wholly different from 'chest': it is about tenderness, nourishment, softness; a different kind of strength, a listening, nurturing strength. It speaks of passion and commitment. Kings and queens have their portraits painted in chest mode; revolutionaries passionately leading their men and unfurling their banners are painted in breast mode. What is this difference? Can the students feel this difference?

As I said, these students are not in their first term. They know each other and I know them and how to partner them up. It is a safe group. Even so, the simple exercise I am about to do can produce tears, laughter, euphoria and everything in between. I tell them this. I remind them that touch is mutual—about giving and receiving—the two cannot be separated; and there is an art in both.

I call over Anna and Claire, and ask Claire to close her eyes. I tell Anna to put her left hand on Claire's chest, so that the palm of the hand rests lightly but firmly on the upper sternum between her breasts (or just above in the case of very busty women, where it is simply not okay to go delving between their breasts and there isn't any room there for there to be any plausible effect). I ask Anna to move her hand in a small slow circle as though she were polishing this area of Claire's chest; not scrubbing, but gently polishing it as though shining the skin until it sparkles. Now, keeping the left hand moving like this, I ask her to put her right hand on Claire's back directly behind the left— i.e. in the middle of the upper back. Now the right hand polishes along with the left. I ask both girls to imagine there is a golden cylinder connecting each of Anna's palms that radiates warmth through Claire's body. The polishing continues in silence for about five minutes. Anna's hands stop moving, but do not lose contact with Claire. Anna applies a little more pressure with her left hand, gently persuading Claire to lean back, and then more pressure with the right to bring her forwards again. She rocks Claire like this for a minute or so and then takes her for a 'walk'; eyes still closed, Claire is walked by Anna holding her this way.

'Feel the connection between the hands!'

Claire opens her eyes.

'In a minute, Anna will let you go. Carry on walking, but guard that sensation of heat back and front.'

Claire walks—and her shoulders are relaxed, her eyes are shining, her mouth is open. A skinny girl, her collarbones have lost their prominence. She is walking with confidence.

'It feels as if I have so much space.'

All the others get into pairs to 'do' each other's chests. Afterwards, I put Jane and Pete opposite each other at a distance of about twelve feet.

'Close your eyes and recall that sensation of heat back and front. Now make eye contact and walk towards each other. Stop when you feel it is appropriate.'

The room is charged. The two approach each other inexorably, beautifully drawn to each other, full, listening, whole. They stop two feet apart and the electricity is jumping between them as the two bodies are communicating silently. This is not about having breasts, but wholehearted openness. To be wholehearted, the chest has to become a breast. It is sensual, beautiful. 'Golly, it's like being in love!' says Pete. No, at that moment, you *are* in love!

I ask them to repeat the exercise, but this time to close down the feeling of warmth, return to chest mode, not to imagine dislike or cold or confrontation, but just to remove the imprint of the partner's hands from their bodies. The magnetism disappears. The sternums are very slightly depressed—not easy to spot, but caution has entered the body, the chins are fractionally further forward, the jaws, fractionally tighter; only a camera would pick it up. The atmosphere has changed. They move towards each other faster, heavier, stop at a greater distance from each other. The tension circles each character rather than buzzing between them. It is a different story. The fences are up.

And this is the crux. We have a chest, but we also have a breast. The actors need to know which they are working with and when. The chest protects, sets up fences, is safe, but it is also hard and solid. The breast is soft, open, listening, but vulnerable. When actors do work requiring a great deal of physical contact, they need to be in breast mode or there is no contact, no development, because there can be no physical dialogue. However, the body is right to have its chest mode: we need protection, and it is the actor's job to move between the two.

'But why does such a simple exercise make such a difference?'

To answer this we have to go back to the realm of child development. Contact aids growth. The right kind of contact provides reassurance, safety, well-being. 'Let me kiss it better' is not just an idle thing mothers say to their children—it works! The contact has a healing property. The above, simple, hands-on exercise can transform a group. The sensitivity between the actors develops remarkably, and as their individual self-confidence grows, the body takes over in the business of listening and communicating.

However, it is not an exercise to be attempted if you have any doubts about the group's 'groupy-ness'. A student may have learned to protect that area very well for any number of reasons pertaining to childhood, hurt, abuse... The teacher must be alert to this and perhaps pair with that student themselves to give a very light dose of the exercise. The work is centred in the part of the body where much is held, and, to someone fragile, it can be painful. Yet we are not doing heavy-duty psychotherapy here: we are simply activating the listening capacity of our bodies through touch, and through releasing the muscles gathered around the powerhouse of the body. When these muscles, the pectoral muscles and their surrounding tissues, are allowed to soften, then the connections between them can be felt. The body is woken up.

*

In the mid-1990s, I worked on a West End show which required three actors to create a three-headed being. 'They need to move as one, but with three separate personalities,' said the director. 'You know, your sort of thing, Christian.' The three actors in question were experienced in the business, and one was something of a soap star. We had a whole morning, and they were keen to show me what they had done: 'But it just doesn't seem to work—we keep falling over each other.' It was the simplest of problems and took me back to making dinosaurs with primary-school children—ten monsters for the tail, and a tail that can move… The problem here was that they were trying to glue themselves together without making contact. They were steeling themselves to connect, with the result that they were 'ham-dram' caricatures *par excellence*. They had not worked with each other prior to rehearsing the play, but the rehearsal process had been going some weeks already. They were experienced actors; a little hands-on work seemed quite appropriate here to make this gluing business more comfortable. We began with some simple exercises and then I moved to my *Breast Versus Chest* exercise. We began, and two of the actors responded very well with an 'Of course,' and proceeded to glue themselves together with ease, moving about as if they had been born like this: 'God, it's simple!'

The soap star, however, stopped the rehearsal. 'I'm leaving. My agent promised me I didn't have to do things like this.' He walked out and the rehearsal ended. The subsequent performance was one of a two-headed monster with a curious appendage, the soap star.

I was saddened and reflected that either he thought this kind of thing silly and unnecessary and saw it as new-age and frivolous (though it's pretty old, really!), or he had had a bad experience of it, which was very possible. Or, finally, the simple act of contact on the chest had touched something that disturbed him and he felt unable to continue. I think this last was the most likely, which saddened me further— for what is movement if not to touch and wake up? An actor, in chest-mode only, is unlikely to develop beyond the soap-star persona. But then that is his choice. This little episode made me more determined to devote at least a term to contact work at LAMDA, and to take contact way beyond the hands and the chest, once trust was established within the group.

Trust Exercises and Contact Work

There is a school of thought that says trust exercises are contact work (which is sometimes literally true), and are very good at bonding a new group of students—good to get students to know each other, get 'groupy', etc. I have had staff at both drama colleges and schools, where I have been a visiting practitioner, say to me: 'Christian, you do that touchy-feely stuff. Can you get our first years to roll over each other a bit? They are awfully nervous of each other.' Possibly with good reason, I reflect, and a bit of roly-poly might make them a whole lot more nervous.

At LAMDA I begin very slowly, and apart from the linking of hands (itself quite an art), I do not do contact in the first term. The students are just beginning the business of working in a group and discovering how to use their bodies. Lying on the floor is enough of a challenge! They have been in the very competitive situation of getting into drama school. Competition still lurks about in that first term, and is dealt with through the gradual discovery of themselves as authors of their movement as a result of being in a group, not despite the group. I even leave the simple eyes-closed trust exercise I described earlier until the second term. There is too much at stake.

I remember going to an audition with a 'physical theatre group'. They needed another actor. At the Diorama Studios I was welcomed by three guys in black leather, chains and leather boots, being fairly physical, and doing lots of bouncing up and down and leg stretches while they introduced each other. You get the picture. 'We work on trust, really,' one said to me, rather vaguely. There were besides these three, four auditionees in the room. I was the only female, and a good foot shorter than the next shortest person there. No problem. We were instructed to hold hands with a partner opposite us—in a line—while an auditionee took a running jump and threw themselves onto our bed of arms. Nice. I was to go first as I'd be 'easy to catch'. 'You know, it's just about freeing up!' Funny how the tension in the room was increasing: arms turning to steel in anticipation and in fear of dropping me. Luckily, young as I was, I didn't take to all these boots and biker stuff and said, 'No, I don't think this is really me.' I left, feeling their pitying glances at my back, and as I reached the bottom of the stairs I heard a suspicious thud.

I mention this episode because some people are mad about trust exercises, and are ready to hurl themselves at anyone and anything. These types have to have an eye kept on them as they would be the first to say, 'Why didn't you catch me?' or, worse, 'What's your problem?' to their terrified partner. Trust exercises are synonymous with contact exercises, but the term 'trust exercise' can inspire this kind of inappropriate daredevilry.

✳

Sophie is in the middle of a group of four actors. In the exercise she is to have her eyes closed and let herself fall in any direction she likes, to be caught by those around her. I am working with a director who loves these kinds of exercises (as do I!), and has got them into groups for some 'go for it' experiences. Sophie's arms are crossed over her chest, her closed eyes are fluttering, and she stands stiff as a board. Her 'catchers' are perilously far away. It must be a bit like the first time you jump off a high-diving board: a bit of a dare. Sophie's steeling herself. Sophie won't have gained anything useful in terms of contact work by this exercise, only the relief of having done it. I wade in.

'No, start again: actors, get much closer to Sophie. No arms allowed. If she begins to lean back, move into her, spread your back under hers, and don't wait for her to fall. Crashing is not allowed. Contact must be constant. Mould yourself to her shape so she can feel the extent of the support. No! Don't curl up ready to support. Move in to her so she can feel it, then continue so you can both travel…'

'Oh, that's so comfortable,' says the relieved Sophie.

I encourage the students to be on the alert: do not wait for a person to fall—anticipate their movement without directing it—move into their movement, and support it in the direction it is going. Appropriate support means the movement can develop between you (perhaps this is the real meaning of 'understanding').

They are still in groups of four: one 'falls', one supports, and two are there for safety. Safety is paramount at this stage: too little confidence or too much are just as dangerous, but not as dangerous as the actor who fails to concentrate for one moment. Now the person falling is supported down to the ground and gently rolls off their partner. As the 'faller's' confidence grows, the pair work more quickly. Then I invite them to 'recall' the feeling of support and fall to the ground. They do so, noiselessly, safely and with astounding fluidity. The physical dialogue between the pair has enabled Sophie to have the confidence to go it alone!

Lettre au Porteur

Contact work is one of the best ways of training one body to read another body with empathy, respect and circumspection. It teaches a body to be *à l'écoute* of another. Where this happens there exists the physical dialogue and where that occurs there is development in acting.

In 1992 I went to see a show in Crawley by Théâtre du Mouvement: *Lettre au Porteur*, performed by Catherine Dubois and the late Lucas Thiery. The show was based on a series of letters written to his girlfriend by a German soldier stationed in Russia during the war. He does not make it home. In the show, his beloved is always present: she is 'on him' for the duration. He is literally carrying the weight of her absence. She never touches the ground. It is as though the memory of her lives on his body—his body is her landscape that unfolds itself under her feet. There are times when he attempts to shake off the memory of her, but her grip tightens and her presence makes footprints on his body. In such physical proximity, there are moments of huge distance, loss, estrangement and solitude. Only when he dies can she leave him, and she does not.

Apart from being one of the most beautiful shows I have ever seen, what struck me was the two bodies constantly adapting to each other: every tiny body movement by one actor had to be accounted for in a transference of weight, a shifting of body parts, by the other. This was not acro-balance (which sometimes is confused with contact improvisation), where trained gymnasts perform fantastic balances between and on each other; this was the most extraordinary, sophisticated adaptability of two bodies that allowed not only the 'conversation on a physical level', but also allowed each actor to become the landscape in which the other could exist. We talk about 'holding a conversation'. Something 'held' can also be dropped, as we know all too painfully when dialogue ceases to happen and argument ensues. The show continued the metaphor, but showed that when dialogue between soldier and beloved stopped—when the conversation was no longer held, the weight of the memory had to be held or both would cease to exist.

Le porteur (the bearer of the letter; literally, 'the carrier') and *le porté* ('the carried') had me hooked. I set off to France to learn this technique with Catherine Dubois, and kept returning to her and joining her *atelier* while I was working at LAMDA.

What is involved in the process of walking over someone else? Catherine Dubois describes the work of *le porté* as an exploration of another's body as though it were an island: the foot has to tread carefully, the senses are alert, but no more than that of *le porteur*, whose body is learning to adapt to the slightest movement of *le porté*. An inclination of the head backwards by *le porté*, unsupported by the musculature of the abdomen and back, can dramatically alter the weight being distributed over *le porteur*.

We have mentioned the effect a handshake can have on another person depending on its quality. Now we have to explore how a foot may step on a body. It has to be an awake foot—a foot as sensitive and responsive as a hand, a flexible, feeling foot. For every step on another person, there has to be time spent in waking the feet up—in putting eyes and ears into them. I have often spent up to an hour on simple foot exercises, going on to simple giving-and-receiving-weight exercises prior to walking over each other. Of course, there are no-go areas, areas where it is inappropriate for a foot to tread: backs of the knees, lower back, breasts, genitals, etc. Stepping on the calves of a prone person requires the feet to follow the line of the calf muscle, not force it inwards, and if those muscles belong to a footballer or cyclist, it is best to steer well clear of them! The transference of weight has to be highly controlled or *le porté* risks collapsing instead of stepping, and *le porteur* will groan accordingly. *Le porté* will produce similar sounds from *le porteur* if she attempts to stand on tiptoe on her partner—forcing her weight into a small area. The work is a challenge to balance and to gravity. A few minutes' work is a strenuous business, but builds strength and stamina very quickly and safely.

Each movement by *le porté* poses the silent question, 'Can I?' which only the body of *le porteur* can answer. So each movement by *le porteur* is an adjustment, but also an offering: 'You may go here.' The body is the imagination here. There can be no preconceived ideas. Initially the students experience a great deal of fear of hurting each other: 'She'll break if I stand on her!' This is why so much time is spent underlining the forbidden zones, getting the students used to taking and giving weight, being totally dependent on one another, working on the feet... Mutual physical respect. I ask one of a pair to walk across the room on her partner's hands only. This is a good way for the pair to adapt to the transference of weight as *le porté* moves to release their partner's hand in order that they may be given a new 'step'.

In pairs I ask the group to create little plays: they have lost each other, are searching for one another and find each other, but all the while conjoined. As they get used to each other's body, stagecraft creeps in: timing, suspension, musicality, and finally, text.

I have used the work of *Porteur/Porté* in much of my staged work and have run workshops in it entitled 'Adapt or die!' It is a vast and wonderful work, but it needs to be taught with plenty of time, by a hands-on and experienced practitioner. It is not something to be toyed with, as it is potentially very dangerous, and the listening qualities it promotes can so easily be turned into strong-arm tactics. Safety has to be the top priority. But safety comes with listening and *Porteur/Porté* has given acting students the skill and confidence to move on to throwing and catching each other with complete confidence.

*

Contact work transforms the body. It strengthens, sensitises, transforms. The body is required to discover the imagination within it, and that imagination is far bigger than that which our brains can supply. Decroux had a walk in which he instructed his students: *'La marche sur le dos de Vénus'* ('The walk on the back of Venus'). A walk of supreme delicacy where the foot practically caressed the ground. Its atmosphere was of extraordinary concentration mixed with total gentleness. The ground became alive. It took a long time to perfect, and was a good walk. But an actor who can walk on another actor literally wakes up that person, and real dialogue ensues—the bodies speak. Contact work is a total work, and as two is greater than one, the benefits double. It further transforms the meaning of 'listening' for the moving actor.

Chapter Eight

The Actor's Voice

Martin and Chloe stand opposite each other in the studio at a distance of about twelve feet. They are to imagine that they are on a damaged railway bridge in the American Midwest. Between them is a frightening gap bridged by a single rail which both pray is strong enough to support their weight. Below is a ravine, and falling means certain death. Martin is the 'father', Chloe the 'child'. Martin is *major*—i.e. he leads the movement. They are to move towards each other, and, on contact, Martin is to bring Chloe back to safety. This is not all; having begun the movement, Martin is to sing his child's favourite lullaby, to help her have the confidence to follow. It is a poignant and dangerous situation.

Martin, a first-year LAMDA student, had been an Oxford choral scholar and has a wonderful voice. He wants to start singing at once and says he has a very good Welsh lullaby. 'Good,' I say, 'but start the movement first.' Martin starts. He wobbles a bit and looks down.

> 'Don't look down,' I say, 'If you lose eye contact with Chloe she won't follow you. You won't be major. Eye contact establishes your relationship. We want to watch both of you, not just you having a wobbly.'

Eye contact is re-established and Martin wobbles along on his 'rail' rather convincingly. Suddenly he stops, draws himself up and looks rather splendid. He is filling up with air and is suddenly very safe.

'Why have you stopped moving across the rail, Martin?'

'I'm about to sing!'

'What about the ravine?'

Martin wobbles a bit more and sings. His body expands gloriously and a wonderful sound comes out. I look round. Some of the audience are whispering, 'I love this song.' I look at Martin; he is in his element. Chloe is unsure what to do. She is standing rather uneasily.

Martin is no longer leading. I cry:

'The rail is breaking—it's splitting!'

Martin looks nonplussed.

'Didn't you like the song?'

'What was more important, your song or bringing Chloe safely over the rails?'

'I don't get it.'

'As soon as you began to sing, your body became safe. We couldn't believe the situation any more. You are a good singer—'

'Er, thanks…'

'—but as soon as you decided to sing "well", you imposed your "singing-well" stance on the body, and the body became heavy; no danger; you forgot Chloe.'

'So my voice should sort of quaver?'

'Not at all, that wouldn't help Chloe much.'

'So…'

'I want to see this terrifying situation of your little girl crossing a ravine on a broken rail and you willing her across with her favourite lullaby.'

'So I must sing soothingly?'

'If you can do that on a rail two hundred feet above a ravine.'

'I don't get it!'

'Martin, when we are watching this, who are we really watching?'

'Chloe.'

'Of course. Your whole being is concentrated on getting Chloe across. Now swap: Chloe, you are the mother singing to Martin, your child.'

'I can't sing very well.'

'Bollocks! Is that what you'd say to your five-year-old stuck out on a rail over a ravine?'

Chloe gives me a long look.

The scene begins. Both bodies tremble. Chloe reaches out her hand towards Martin and gingerly moves forwards. We hold our breath. She is clearly very frightened, but her eyes are fixed on Martin, she smiles, and he follows.

'Now!' I whisper, and Chloe sings without stopping her approach. When it feels very dangerous, she pauses and then continues. Her voice does not falter, but nor is it safe. It is an utterly open sound directed entirely at Martin, clear as a bell. The tension is huge—will they fall? The poignancy is overwhelming, because we can see what the 'child', Martin, cannot see—i.e. the danger they are both in. They reach each other and the audience gasp with relief.

'Chloe, that was the most beautiful sound.' I ask the audience to remember the words of Martin's lullaby. They all have the tune, but can't remember the words. What about Chloe's song? They remember every word though they have never heard it before. She'd made it up. Everyone is perplexed.

'Don't you see the difference between Martin and Chloe in this exercise was that Martin was preparing to sing whereas Chloe was acting; she was in the moment in the play.'

'Yes, but I'm never doing that again,' says Chloe.

'Why not? You were wonderful.'

'I hate heights.'

Martin tries again. This time he shows the rail to be even more dangerous. He is trying very hard. When he begins to sing this intensifies and his voice quavers hysterically.

'Martin, this is selfish.'

'Why?'

Martin is crestfallen (he is one of the most unselfish of students).

'Because you hogged the stage. Where was Chloe?'

Something is dawning, and I change the scenario. Did Martin have a baby brother or sister. Yes?

'Remember your mum getting her off to sleep?'

'Oh God, it was awful!'

'Now imagine you have got her off to sleep with your lullaby. The room you are in has creaky boards. You must leave the room but continue singing the lullaby until you are safely out of it—or she just might wake up.'

Chloe curls up in the middle of the floor, 'baby-fashion'. She is primed to wriggle or scream should Martin's voice become heavy or histrionic.

This time Martin is one hundred per cent in the play. His voice is different: soft, clear, beautiful. We never forget the baby.

'Well done! How does your voice feel?'

'Oh, fine—I didn't think about it. I was too pre-occupied with Chloe not waking up.'

This is the first time Martin has let the play direct his singing, and not let his will to sing well take precedence.

I remind students that quality of movement, or perhaps it would be better to say quality of movement-play, dictates the quality of voice. Voice is the extension of the play: it is the vocal expression of the intention in the play. It is not a mirror to the movement, as in wobbly movement equals wobbly voice (though that can be fun). If this is recognised then the voice is free. However, 'intention' is not 'will', and the two must not be confused. This is something that interests me greatly when working on the connection between movement and voice. When an actor uses willpower he risks isolating himself within a scene. Martin was, in the first exercise, determined to sing well. He forgot that the intention, his intention, in the play was to save Chloe. He concentrated on singing well and the drama was lost. His body became secure, and the dramatic situation collapsed. His will, his determination to sing well, blocked the movement-voice connection. It made him deaf to the play. Will blocks, but intention allows something new to be discovered, another quality, because it is about reaching out into the situation.

I also tell the students that whatever constraints the actor's body is put under by the drama he is inhabiting, the voice is always free. Unless someone has their hands around his throat and stops his air passages, the voice, of itself, can come to no harm. It is when the actor separates movement-play and voice in an acting situation, when they stop acting in order to sing, stop playing in order to declaim, that the voice is usually in trouble.

Making the connection between movement and voice is something I work on with students in their very first term of training. I feel it is crucial that they see right from the start that voice and movement have to be part of an integrated whole, because it is only when this happens that both can be absolutely free.

I am not a voice teacher and I have limited understanding of vocal folds and uvulas, unlike my expert colleagues in the voice department. But I cannot be a movement teacher without understanding breathing and acting. When working on specific techniques such as dance and fight, as a rule the voice is not part of that discipline, but in the acting situation the voice can no more be separated from the actor than movement can.

In the bad old days in the mid-1980s, I was often asked by theatre directors to take so-and-so out of rehearsal to work on their movement in a particular scene. 'Don't bother about the text,' I was told, 'it's the movement I'm worried about.' There was a cut-and-paste attitude to the purpose of movement, an expectation that voice and movement were somehow added on to acting or sort of fixed individually. Of course, there is some truth in this: an actor may be having trouble with the steps at a particular moment, but everything depends on everything else, and I can no more exclude voice from my work than ask an actor to remove his head.

Élan and Text

A voice class is a physical business. You will see actors leaning against walls to open up the chest, legs lowered to the floor whilst on their back as 'sh'—'mm'—'phaw' sounds are articulated. Many of our exercises overlap. For example, the body has to learn to relax in both classes. In the movement class, relaxation may happen through breathing techniques or the performing of tiny movements. The purpose is to allow the muscle groups to relax so that students can feel the difference between tense muscles, muscles in tension, and muscles that have released their tenseness. It is a vital part of learning to listen to the body.

Voice teachers, equally, need a relaxed and listening body before they can begin to explain how the speaking/singing actor can function best, how they can start to develop the notion of breath unconstrained by tense muscles or bad postural habits. Lying on the floor does not of itself produce relaxation and can be quite an uncomfortable business. I will tend to use tiny movements on the floor to aid the body to let go, as well as using breathing techniques. Where there are particular blockages and a student has little or no sense of parts of their body, I ask them to enjoy singing gently into those areas. If you hold a sheet of paper in your hand whilst music is being played, the paper will vibrate. So your muscles will vibrate as you gently feed sound in their direction. A vibrating muscle is an awake muscle, and only when a muscle is awoken can it hear that it may relax. Voice and movement complement each other in this business of preparing the actor for work. Yet when we stand up and 'act', this wholeness has a tendency to vanish.

During my student days I was fascinated by the French word '*élan*' that I have already talked about in Chapter Five. Philippe Gaulier, one of the most extraordinary theatre teachers of our generation (and one who has probably never led a voice warm-up in his life), would talk about the voice following the *élan* of the movement. *Élan* is 'flight', 'impetus', a 'start', a 'spring'. It is the springboard. In the action of throwing, it is the physical intent behind the moment of throwing. For example, when throwing a ball to another, the quality of the *élan* will direct the ball in order that it may be caught satisfactorily. As the ball leaves the hand there is a moment of suspension—the body is caught in stillness as the thrower waits to see if the ball has reached its mark. In this moment, the quality of the *élan* is held, its intention is so strong that it causes the observer to take their eyes from the thrower to the catcher. A natural progression. It was in this moment of suspension that Philippe Gaulier has us speak. Now many vocal exercises get the student to speak on the *élan* of movement. I remember brandishing and swinging a huge teapot for Barbara Bridgmont as she got me to do *Hiawatha*—to find the physical beat of the poem—but with Philippe the *élan* was part of a game just as throwing a ball is, which meant we never forgot the other players.

One of his favourite and one of his hardest exercises was to have us imagine we were on the stage in a huge theatre. We had to sing a lullaby, but our intention was to sing it to one special person high up in the gods—miles away. We were given a soft ball and had to hurl it up in 'their' direction, and hold the body in suspension as the ball left our hand. We had to 'see' the ball rising higher and higher in an arc towards our beloved up there. With the effort of throwing the ball so far, you might expect an enormous sound to emerge from the *élan*, but only if you took the exercise literally. The voice follows the *intention* of the *élan*, and the intention is to sing a *lullaby* to someone far away. You do not shout a lullaby, yet with the body poised in this way, every cell intent on reaching the beloved, then the lullaby is a pure clear sound that can be heard miles away. When the suspension wobbles, when the actor uses his voice to compensate for the failing suspension, then the lullaby is lost. We are always amazed by the actor who can sing or speak very quietly but whose every word is audible. The point here is that the movement-play of the *élan*—i.e. the intention behind and the quality of the throwing of the ball—allows the actor to discover a new and utterly truthful sound that is supported by the whole body in play.

The Problem of Noise

'I hate it when actors shout!' This is something you often hear from critics, audience members, your mother… We all hate shouting—it has nasty overtones of domestic chaos, tears before bedtime and sore throats. But is it the fact of actors shouting or the noise they are making that we object to, because shouting doesn't automatically mean 'stick your fingers in your ears'? I have worked with the army on vocal presentation, and it is interesting that what happens there is an extreme of what can happen in the actor's situation. If you are a captain it is not easy to get an order across to a bunch of men while you are in uniform, in boots that are uncomfortable, standing ramrod straight and with the head tilted slightly back (a peculiar feature of the army which in the 'stand to attention' setting is physically disabling), and get that order across, outside. The sound that emerges can be forced and furious. It is one born of tenseness. It is exhausting to produce, and the loud sound becomes synonymous with anger and effort. The sound is unsupported by the body and the term 'strangled sound' is very apt indeed.

This kind of shouting can do untold damage to the voice: for the captain, the vocal folds are under as much tension as they can be. As a result they are not free to meet and beat together in the flow of air, i.e. the out-breath. Thus, the air escapes unused for the purpose of making a sound. To gain any power the voice has then to be used with controlled violence; the resulting explosive outbursts of air cause the folds to react convulsively and produce the rasping sound so much associated with the parade ground. This kind of sound has little or no resonance and resonance-less sounds (rather like fingernails dragged down the blackboard) are usually unbearable sounds. No wonder we can't stand screaming soldiers or actors for any length of time.

When using movement to deal with the shouting problem for both actors and soldiers, I never start with the problem. I start with a game. Focusing on the problem, in my experience, is rarely helpful. It tends to frustrate and embarrass. Much better to solve the problem through diversion as you would a child's tantrum.

The 'Yes!' Exercise

I line the students up and have them gaze far over my head. This is easier if you happen to be working in a studio with a high ceiling. One of LAMDA's rehearsal spaces was a Victorian church—gloomy, but plenty of height to play with. The game is that the students are gazing up at a window at which sits their beloved. Like Rapunzel's tower, the window is high up. The beloved has been refusing to go out for weeks, but has suddenly changed his or her mind and actually asked you out. In ecstasy (students love that bit), you throw a present up to the creature in the window and shout 'Yes!' in a way to make the very bricks reverberate. The quality of the *élan* here will dictate the quality of the voice, and usually students produce a wonderful resonating sound—very loud and very bearable. However, here again, if the acting student decides or wills a loud sound, the voice screams and the body becomes smaller in the space. The 'present' drops on the floor. The sound causes the other students to put their hands over their ears.

'What are you doing?'
'Making a loud sound.'
'No, you are throwing a present to your beloved.'
'Oh, I forgot.'

'What is she wearing?'

'I dunno.'

'Look.'

'Oh, um, jeans and something else.'

I provoke the poor boy until he really 'sees' the beloved. He had forgotten the play, the intention behind the play. The intention provided him with the *élan* that would free the voice.

Some actors are so trapped in the screaming thing that no amount of imaginative scenarios will help. With these actors (and they are usually very fine actors), a different tactic is needed: physical diversion. One of the things I do is to place the actor at the back of the studio, and place my hands on his or her shoulders. The actor has to push me across the room while speaking to the beloved up in their window. I provide a strong resistance, and can always enlist help. The more they are physically resisted, the more determined the actor becomes to push me away. This intensifies when I place a human 'beloved' up on a stool at the opposite end of the studio. This actor has their back to the actor I am restraining and by now knows only to turn and 'hear' when the rich full and free sound is heard. The restrained actor's body is working one hundred per cent, every inch of it in a working tension—totally focused on getting me out of the way. We usually end up exhausted on the floor, but the voice has found a new resonance, a freedom and volume that is exciting and very loud. 'How's the voice?' 'Oh, it's fine, but I'm knackered.' The voice is always free. The actor had finally entered into the game.

Occasionally this just does not happen. The actor is fixed on shouting unbearably. This is not a voice problem as such, but more a mental judgement that cannot be shifted at once. With these actors (and soldiers!), great delicacy is required. No responsible teacher will ever endure an uncontrolled scream for even a second, and with experience a teacher can even anticipate that sound, and prevent it completely. Here a different kind of diversion is needed, which I shall talk about later when talking about freeing text.

The 'Yes' Exercise, among many others, aims to produce a rich, resonant sound. Students ask me how they can get that quality of sound without the *élan*, without hurling imaginary presents around the studio. The answer has a lot to do with body-memory.

Philippe Gaulier introduced me to a hilarious exercise that I have extended and adapted again and again when working with first-year students. It goes like this:

Football and Watch-mending

An actor is to stand near the far end of the studio. He is in training on the football ground. At the other end is his deaf grandfather sitting on a bench. Four fellow actors line up with soft balls and hurl them at our person in training—at a height where he has to jump to hit them back. There is no let up, the balls are thrown and collected and thrown again continually. While our actor 'trains' in this way, he tells his deaf grandfather how to make leek soup.

It is a most exhausting game, but hitting the balls provides the *élan* for the voice, so it opens, and we get the volume coming from a free and relaxed place. I give the actor a minute's rest: 'I'm shattered!' 'How's the voice?' 'Oh, fine thanks.' Then the process is repeated, but the balls are mimed. Usually this has better results than the hitting of the real balls. The actor thoroughly enters the play and becomes the most powerful and skilful whacker of balls!

Now I make this thoroughly panting actor sit on a chair. He is a watch-mender, and is to mime the mending of the Lord Mayor's watch—a very delicate and intricate business. This is his profession, and he is very competent at it. In the back room is grandfather again, deaf as a post. The actor is to tell his grandfather about the evening's supper menu while he works. It can become a wonderfully comic play. I always put some 'grandfather' in the background who inevitably mishears and misunderstands. I ask the actor to recall the huge sound he made in football training when he speaks to his grandfather in this new scenario.

He patiently repeats himself again and again in a great booming voice. His focus is on his watch. If the actor resorts to anger, and forces the voice, the watch is destroyed. Loud sound does not equal anger, and the actor holds the memory of his 'training' voice in his body so he can achieve the most delicate and intricate of tasks whilst producing a free, open sound. The scene could continue for ages. No one is exhausted. But if the actor forgets the play, forgets he has been having to shout at his grandfather, whom he loves very much, for over ten years, he risks hurting his voice.

During feedback I remind the actors of their intentions: in the 'training' scenario, the intention of the actor was to tell grandfather how to make leek soup whilst he was training. It was not to do training whilst talking to his grandfather. He is not willing his grandfather to learn how to make leek soup. He wants to get his training done—that is his primary intention. It just happens grandfather is on the pitch after a recipe. That is the play. Similarly, on the chair, his intention is to tell grandfather about supper whilst mending a watch. He doesn't screw up a watch every time he talks to grandfather. That is a different play.

To demonstrate this latter point further, I ask the students to stand in a wide circle. They have a ball that is thrown around the circle from actor to actor. The game is to say the name of the actor to whom you are throwing the ball with a given emotion. I name the emotions—e.g. love, hope, passion, jealousy, etc. When it comes to the more so-called negative emotions—i.e. Anger and hate—the ball is invariably dropped, because it is thrown without care. It is no longer a game. If an actor remembers to play anger, he is still playing the game, and his body and his voice are totally free when playing. The actor who shouts unbearably has not learned to play. Willing anger or willing loudness is very different from intending anger or loudness within a play, and has very different results when it comes to a student actor's development of vocal technique.

Losing the 'Way of Doing'

I was twenty-eight when I discovered the voice work of Enrique Pardo, and for the next four years went to any and every workshop he was giving. I was becoming more and more interested in the success of diversion tactics involved in movement training, and here was Enrique with a lovely system of diversion tactics he was using to free the voice. My favourite was the use of a character he calls '*l'Ange qui dérange*'—literally, the 'disturbing angel'. An actor delivering their text would be disturbed or gently tormented by another. Resistance to the angel was not allowed, and by gradually yielding physically and mentally to the angel, the actor would often find they were able to lose themselves completely, and the text became full of new and extraordinary qualities now it was 'loosened'.

Of course, the actor in question might have found a very splendid way in which to deliver the text. But when a 'Way of Doing' a text is discovered—a 'WOD' as I call it—it can be problematic. A text used for a recording or an audition, isolated from the context of the play that is itself an ever-changing beast, can imprison an actor. The WOD becomes a costume you cannot remove. The problem for the actor is that they don't necessarily know they can't take it off. Let me give you an example.

Tanya, an actor several years out of drama school, has prepared Juliet's 'Gallop apace, you fiery-footed steeds!' What she does is very beautiful, very clear and full of passion, but rather earnest. Good for the audition, but perhaps not so good for the fourteen-year-old Juliet. I ask her to do it again, and I see the exact copy of the previous rendition, word for word, gesture for gesture. I ask her to deliver the text to Jack, an actor sitting next to me, and to say his name whenever I click my fingers. I do this to try and interrupt her 'Way of Doing' the text. Now we have a sort of schizophrenic performance where Jack is frequently addressed in a new tone, but Tanya reverts to her WOD immediately she is back to the text. Jack says it makes him feel peculiar as the text doesn't seem to be addressed to him at all.

I get Tanya to lie down on some cushions: 'Just do the text to Jack from the cushions. No need to work.' Tanya is very pleased, but relax? Good God, no! When she opens her mouth the head comes forward from the cushions, the gestures creep back in exactly as before. She is like a record that has got stuck; her body is imprisoned by her WOD. The text refuses to give. It cannot. The WOD has come from the mind and forced itself on the body. The body is following every phrase with gesture and posture, often very appropriate and beautiful, but stuck. Tanya has not produced a text and then done the dreadful business of gluing gestures onto it. No, she has lived the text, felt it in her bones, but then sealed it in aspic.

I often tell actors that imagination is in the body: rather than being limited to a space in the brain, it lies in the movements of fingers and toes, in the contraction and relaxation of muscles. In improvisation, imagination is the response of the body to space, time, music and human dynamic that fuels the thinking brain, not the other way round. The body is the prime motor. So deciding how the body should react during delivery of a text limits both the actor's movement and freezes the text delivery in a 'version'. Tanya has a good version, but not one that responds to the space. It is not alive.

Tanya's audience likes it. 'That's good, Tan...' I ask them what the speech was about.

> 'Oh, you know—it's famous. I can't remember, but God, didn't she look good!'

I ask Tanya to do the text again, still addressing it to Jack. Now we employ *l'Ange qui dérange*: a third actor enters the space and attempts to distract Tanya from delivering her text to Jack. Tanya is not allowed to resist, nor must the angel totally distract her—only when her WOD is getting the upper hand. This 'angel' is my physical prop. I could have told Tanya a million times and in a million different ways to 'relax', 'let go', 'get angry', 'soften', etc., but when a WOD has really got hold of an actor, then physical intervention is necessary in order to set free the body's imagination.

The 'angel' gently shakes her, tickles her, prods her. Tanya doesn't like it. She is not allowed to resist, yet she must get that text over to Jack. She becomes angry, uses every tactic to escape the angel. She is becoming exhausted, and the angel stops her mouth. She is relieved of the pressure of speaking. Her muscles visibly relax. Her physical version of the text disappears. The angel lets her continue, and the WOD rushes back. I suggest the angel sits on Tanya, on her upper back and gently presses her head onto the floor. Tanya doesn't know whether to laugh or cry. 'Do your text, Tanya,' I say. Again, she tries to lift her head. The WOD is so strong, but she gives up. The whole body collapses. The tension goes. She opens a hand.

'Where's Jack?'

'I'm here.'

She speaks her text, clear, open, free. The body has yielded. The angel took her body on a journey. The body was constrained in many ways, but now Tanya has given up, given way. Cars give way at the 'Give Way' signs in order that another car may pass. Tanya has allowed something else to happen: by yielding, she has released her WOD, and the voice can come from another place. The mind has released its grip. The audience listens to every word, rapt. The voice was always free, but Tanya's mental 'understanding' of the text, her version of it, her WOD, imprisoned both body and voice.

Embodying Text

The voice is always free. We have established that. It is the combination of the mind and inappropriate tense muscles that promotes vocal damage; the mind that wills sound without awareness from a tense body that cannot support it. The body is tense and therefore not at ease. The actor is working with 'dis-ease', if you like. Tenseness must not be confused with tension here. Tension is alive, it breathes (the hands of the watch-mender in the last exercise are in tension or he wouldn't do his job properly; if they were tense he would have given up the profession years ago). Tenseness is about blocking, about fear. Where there is undue tenseness there is usually no play. When the body is fully inhabited, however, when it plays and listens without judgement, then the voice has its chance to expand and develop. It can play too.

Singing used to accompany manual work. In a way the actor now needs work to accompany singing. Many teachers of voice and movement will put their students in a circle, and in unison they all 'dig'. This is a whole-body movement. One 'digger' shouts/sings a phrase, e.g. 'Ye-e-oh', and the rest repeat the phrase as a chant in rhythm with the digging. Any digger can lead, and the leadership changes. What is important is that the digging gets done. If an actor tries to be complicated with their phrase, or thinks more about their 'turn', then the digging, the entire game, will fall apart. When the body is fully engaged in the play of 'digging together', the most 'I can't sing' actor will produce a marvellous and marvellously unexpected sound. Here we go again—when the body is fully engaged in the playing of an activity, lost in it, in fact, the voice is loosened. We talk about being 'lost in thought', and by that we mean the subject has entered a new space. So it is physically.

Peter Bridgmont in his excellent little volume *The Spear Thrower* (An Grianán) writes:

> When we read, what we are doing is to translate the words on the printed page into thoughts. Unless we soon translate the thoughts into deeds by, say, moving or dancing the thoughts, they become over-attached to the 'head process'.

He goes on to say that when thoughts have to be declaimed, they have to become 'active'. He suggests many brilliant exercises to activate thoughts in order that eventually the actor may reach a point when they can speak the text in absolute stillness, but the words will retain the movement of dance within them.

I get an actor to sway gently from right to left to help centre the body and find the central axis. In the same way, the voice needs to be carried by, travel with and be felt by the body going in hundreds of directions, before finding that richness that stands free from empty gesture and illustration. The voice comes from a whole body that moves or has moved as a whole. It is the duty of the movement teacher to take the actor's body on that journey.

*

Actors are complex people: what works for one in terms of releasing the text may not work for another. Two actors, Paul and Maria, came to me for four days' exploratory work prior to devising their own physical-theatre show. Highly skilled physical performers, they shared the problem experienced by many actors who have not had any formal voice training, or who put physicality above voice in terms of theatrical importance. These two could make very funny sounds, funny little voices, cartoon voices, wonderful imitations of corks being pulled from bottles of wine and then of the wine pouring into a glass. Very clever. Yet when it came to truthful vocal expression from the heart, they were stuck. Now these two had no written text, but had a very clear idea of the characters they wanted to work on: he a sea captain, she his widow. Paul had a good idea of his character from the sort of sideburns the captain wore to the way he planted his feet on the ground.

'Well,' I asked, 'did he die at sea?' Paul didn't know, hadn't decided. To me it was clear his character was not embodied, yet. He could describe him, give him gestures, but he wasn't 'in' him, and so couldn't play him. I longed to improvise around the subject, but time was short, and I wanted these two to go away with something concrete to work from.

Paul had a tendency to become a bit of a Peter Pan character whenever he improvised. He was in his fifties and a good six feet tall so this became somewhat inappropriate and unbearable. This was his 'Way of Doing' which surfaced at every improvisation, and he was utterly imprisoned by it, as I had been by my 'arm thing', years ago, in training.

I sat him on a chair and asked him to have a space between his teeth—enough to hold a cigarette in. This immediately softened his jaw and neck, while calming the somewhat manic Peter Pan gleam from his eyes. I asked him to imagine that the distance from his chin to his coccyx was very, very long. He was to imagine heavy boots and laces. Crucially, he was to keep the level of his nose and chin slightly higher than his eye level. In his sternum was a softness, the softness of a newly hatched chick. I continued to make tiny alterations to his posture. I was going to interview him, and

I instructed him to swallow before answering any of my questions.

I asked simple questions at first: name, age, etc. The answers were immediate. Then I pressed for details about his ship. The ship was masterfully described. Here was a captain who knew his ship. Was there a wreck? There was. Whose fault? No answer. Whose fault? I insisted. Nothing. I asked him to gaze into the distance and there see the deck—his first mate, the crew...

'What are they doing?'

'Playing cards.'

'Are they all there?'

Paul shifted his posture slightly. There was a Peter Pan moment. Paul the actor was thinking, making judgements.

'Yes, they are.'

'You are lying!' I was furious. Paul, startled, went straight back to the posture I'd given him.

'Yes, sorry.'

Gradually a grim, moving tale of sabotage, insurrection and betrayal emerged. Paul was extraordinary: his voice had become deep and gentle—the pain of the captain's experiences gradually unfolding. He had found his character. By playing my game, by totally entering a new physique (though one only marginally different from his own), his body had entered a world where every gesture and utterance made was truthful because it was embodied.

This game, if we can call it a game, is very akin to mask work: the face in mask work is replaced by a new shape, a new expression. It is literally constrained by the presence of this new shape, and the constraint allows the body a freedom and energy perhaps undiscovered hitherto.

'When you lied, what was happening?'

'Oh, that chick thing, that softness, in the sternum wasn't there. I was guessing what would be right.'

Shortly after this I was working with fifteen talented actors on texts they had brought with them. Anna, a beautiful actor, lovely voice and fabulous figure, stepped forward. Her chosen text, tough or brave depending, was 'Romeo, Romeo, wherefore art thou Romeo?' While she delivered this small speech she planted herself in the space, made fists of her hands, and let her eyes shine. She looked splendid, but the veins stood out on her neck and her collarbones were curiously prominent.

There was a great deal of tenseness. I asked the audience for feedback.

'Great eyes.'

'What was she saying?'

'Oh, everyone knows what she was saying. It's old hat.'

'What was she saying to you?'

Here is the same old problem. The speech looks extraordinary, it sounds good, Anna has found a WOD that works for her, but it has not been *heard*.

'Well, of course you don't expect people to understand every bit of Shakespeare.'

Lawks! I think of the many plays in foreign languages I have not understood, but that have spoken to the core of my being. I tell the students that understanding exactly what the text means is not the issue. If you feel you have understood a text you often risk limiting its possibilities. What is important is to feel the shape of the text, its music, the perceived intention in the text. Then, instead of concentrating on the outcome, you concentrate on what it is coming out of.

I seat Anna on a table, feet swinging. I ask her to sit on her hands. I then ask her to draw her chin in an inch or two, and chew some imaginary gum. The veins and collarbones disappear. What was her favourite food when she was around twelve or thirteen? Her legs stop swinging.

'Swing your legs.'

'Ice-cream soda.'

'Close your eyes. I'm going to give you an ice-cream soda.'

'Goody.'

'Where do you feel that pleasure.'

'In my sternum, sort of light and squishy.'

'Look over there and open your eyes. Keep chewing! You see the ballroom, your parents, the party. What is Lady Capulet wearing?'

'Leopard skin.'

'Where is your father?'

'He's seeing out an unwanted guest.'

'How do you know?'

'He's got that look which means "get out".'

'Does it frighten you?'

'Oh, never.'

'Why not?'

'I never upset him.'

'Is there anybody you want to talk to in the ballroom?'

'Oh yes! He's wonderful. I've never seen him before. He's heavenly!'

'Where's Tybalt?'

'Fuck Tybalt! I want to talk to Romeo.'

'But where is Tybalt?'

'Oh, somewhere about.' Legs stop swinging.

'I think you know where he is. Swing your legs.'

Anna swings her legs and colours. She is uncomfortable.

'What do you see?'

'He's near me, watching me.'

'Is he in love with you?'

'Yes, no, I don't know. I just wish he'd go away.'

'Look at Romeo—do your text.'

As though set free from the constraints of the ballroom, the text comes out fresh, young. It is not stuck any more.

This process can go on and on, yet I never let it go beyond twenty minutes. It requires enormous concentration on my part, watching every little movement: is the actor in the 'body' I have given him or her, or are they allowing their judgement gradually to creep in and let the mind take over. Whether or not we like Juliet chewing gum and swinging her legs is not the issue here. I have given Anna a shape, a way of being to hold on to. This has saved her body (a greater source of imagination than the mind) from being dictated to by her understanding, her version of the text. It has given her a new costume that allows her voice an embodied freedom.

'What did she say?' I ask the audience again. They all start at once and practically do the whole speech. She was heard.

Method acting? No. Stanislavsky's 'Given Circumstances'? Given *physical* circumstances—yes. It might need the tiniest physical adjustment to release actors from their WOD, and when found and maintained, the possibilities are endless.

After all, Chaplin did not follow a prescribed route in order to discover the tramp. He did not have an 'idea' of the tramp. He found a costume and the rest is history.

*

When I look back over what I have talked about, the key word, again, is 'play'. All actors can speak. Most actors can sing, though not all actors are singers. Most actors can make a text come alive and be fresh each time it is spoken. The problems arise when body and thought are not integrated, when the body becomes the prison of an idea instead of giving birth to it.

Does thought provoke the body, or the body the thought? I'll finish by considering the hungry baby: the smile has gone from the six-week-old baby. He begins to tremble, and then almost propels himself out of his mother's arms as he arches backwards. Now his colour changes from a gentle pink to puce to purple; eyes disappearing, his mouth opens wide. Now we get it, the furious ear-splitting howl that can go on minute after minute, hour after hour. That little person's huge voice never gets hoarse or croaky. No glycerine drops for that baby or any other.

The whole of the baby's body is involved in the business of screaming. It is a whole-body experience, voice and body inextricably linked, as of course they are. The voice is part three of a basic situation. Baby is hungry, tummy signals go to the brain, brain signals the whole muscular system to prepare to boom. The boom is the social bit. No need to boom if we were motherless baby turtles. Was any part of the baby *not* involved in his tantrum? We, as actors, can learn a lot from this.

Chapter Nine

Musicality and Visual Spacing

A Question of Choreography or Acting

Autumn 1998. 'Can you make this bunch look good?' I am working with director John Retallack on *A Midsummer Night's Dream* for the Oxford Theatre Company. The cast of twelve look at me expectantly. We are about to rehearse Act II, Scene I, Puck's entrance, and John wants all the cast onstage: the humans are to inhabit a different time zone from the fairies. They are to be 'dreaming' as we watch the meeting between Puck and the 'Spirit'.

I know I can arrange the actors to look marvellous, and I do. We could take a snapshot of this moment, stick it in the programme, blow it up and hang it outside the theatre. That would draw the audiences in. 'Terrific, Christian, thanks a million.' I am dismissed, but have my doubts. Can the actors carry on 'looking good' through the scene? What will sustain them—there is no music, no choreography. Well, they are actors, and there is nothing unusual about having the whole cast onstage at once...

To sustain 'looking good', actors are told, rightly, that thought and intention are paramount, as are 'focus' (that peculiarly nebulous term) and 'presence' (an even more nebulous acting term!). What is the thought, though, in Lysander's head when he is required to be either absolutely stock-still for an entire scene, or move slowly in a dream-like trance providing a backdrop for the fairies? I think John wants them to look like a beautiful mobile, but what then is the 'wind' that moves the mobile? Of course, as far as I'm concerned, it is musicality.

I have devised many shows and movement-directed many others. Many of the shows have had a cast of up to thirty onstage all the time. That old, overused saying, 'There are no small parts, only small actors', is very true here, because even if only a couple of your thirty actors are absent for a rehearsal, the space is immediately unbalanced. It doesn't matter that those two have no lines or are just 'present', what is important is that they are needed for their contribution to a musical whole: they affect the stage and the other actors. There is a crucial harmony present that is independent of the instructions or directions of choreography. (Remember we are not talking about dance here.)

The day after I have 'placed' John's actors, he is anxious. 'It looked so good, but then somehow didn't. Why couldn't they have just carried on looking good? They all knew what the scene was about...' I ask John for an hour with the actors, not to look at the scene, but to play. 'Yes, yes, I think we've got time.' (So unusual in rehearsals!) John is brilliant at becoming invisible on these occasions. He crawled into a seat at the back of the studio and disappeared, watching us all the time. We play an invaluable game I learned from Enrique Pardo, and have used on countless occasions. Enrique uses it mainly as a means of loosening up actors into 'losing' and 'loosening' their texts (see the previous chapter). As a way of getting actors to really understand the business of space and spacing onstage, it's fantastic.

Leading and Following

The actors begin in pairs: one is leader and the other follows. But this is not 'follow my leader'. For a start, the leader must never look directly at the follower, and vice versa. The following has to be simultaneous with the leading—no perceptible time-lag is allowed. If the leader jumps onto a table, then the follower has to jump onto a table at the same time. If there is no table handy, then the follower must still jump and follow the dynamic of the leader's movement. This is the key: it is not about mirroring or copying the leader, it is about being the leader's dynamic twin. As far as an audience is concerned, it should not be possible to tell who is leading and who is following.

At first there are difficulties. Both the leader (A) and the follower (B) steal glances at each other. They wish to be doing their thing correctly. This sabotages the game as we immediately see the covert relationship between the two. I tell the Bs to have a secret subtext: 'I can actually do what you, leader, can do—better in fact, even if I don't know what you are doing.' This is not to make B upstage A, but be in synch with A—just as a violin and clarinet would be in a duet, though making entirely different sounds.

'Help! I've lost sight of my leader.'

'Lucky you! You cannot look for your leader, so stand still. Hold the space. You have not been abandoned—actually, you are free from ties—it's just that you can't continue until your leader comes into your field of vision.'

'I feel like a lost sheep.'

'Yes, but look where you are—centre stage! How about that?'

'Cripes—what shall I do?'

'Nothing! Enjoy being centre stage without having to do anything.'

'Oh… Yeah… Cool!'

With ten or so pairs working at once, difficulties present themselves that are the best part of the game. For example, Jane's follower Mark has Ed right in his path. Ed is still: he is Josh's abandoned follower. Mark can only move around Ed if Jane does a 'moving round' movement that Mark can follow. Otherwise there are two options: one, to stop in front of Ed and continue following Jane on the spot with arms and legs; or, more interestingly, two, take Ed with him. Followers are passive in the sense they can be moved about like this, but they do not become someone else's follower as a result. Ed can easily be retrieved by Josh reappearing in his line of vision. In this way, there is no conflict or resistance between pairs—just ingenuity and spatial awareness. Jane might grab Ed round the middle, tight. Josh, seeing what has happened to his partner, might perform a sort of rock 'n' roll twist: Ed follows the twisting movement and thereby releases himself from Jane's embrace.

The players begin to get the hang of it. I now put them in threes: one leader, two followers. The followers can place themselves anywhere in the studio, and follow from there—and, indeed, from any physical position they happen to choose. The encounters between the groups are now more complex—there is more for both leaders and followers to consider.

I choose three groups of three. Three leaders. They are in charge of their own group, but they are also in charge of the space and of us, the audience. They now need to know which group or individual is the focus at any given time. They need to see if the stage is balanced, if the rhythm of the movement is samey, confusing, or has sent the audience to sleep. They need to know exactly which follower(s) have been 'lost', and whether these 'lost' souls are providing a new focus for the game. They need to make sure the stage is anchored from time to time—i.e. That there is a degree of stillness amongst some of the actors in order for others to be seen.

The game takes time and practice. I need to change the groups around, choose different leaders. Sometimes the energy becomes sluggish—no one is daring to pick up the reins. I give them some music. Disaster! The leaders start moving to the music—a rather bad dance is happening. The leadership becomes wispy and there is no drama, only anaemic movement. Music before they move is better. It gives them a buzz, an atmosphere to work with or against. The real music has to be inside their bodies, in their composition of the space, in their listening to its rhythm.

The stage might be utterly still. Then one leader makes a sudden movement, crouching to the ground. His followers do the same movement; the other leaders might remain still, watching where this may go, letting us watch it… or they may all join the movement… or… There are musical choices which in their turn are dramatic. The space is alive and watchable without music, text or even a story.

A common problem is 'easy movement'. The leaders sometimes feel that they must make their movement easy to follow. It can become bland, symmetrical, or of one rhythm; 'Movement' with a capital M. It can resemble a lot of rather sickly parades: majorettes, or worse, Hitler Youth, without even the band to alleviate the obviousness of it. It is quite alarming how groups can get high on easy movement like this.

> 'Stop—anchor the stage. Try and be difficult to follow. Be eccentric. No one wants to follow an eccentric— especially into battle!'

Enrique Pardo called quirky leadership of this kind, 'tacit leadership'. Quiet leadership, leadership that is sometimes downright unsatisfactory to follow.

I now give the followers a choice. Within the spirit of the game, they may change leaders. In this way, a leader or even two leaders can be isolated creating new and dramatic stories for the audience.

Of course, there is no planned story. There cannot be. But the acute observation of both leaders and followers means that every actor is responsible for the play, the design, and the musicality of the stage. It is not a question of awaiting a turn or passing the focus between the actors. The game involves everyone all the time—even, or rather, especially, in the moments of greatest stillness. The game gives the actors authenticity: they become authors of a composition, not instruments in a work of choreography.

This is the game I play with John's actors for an hour. They get the hang of it pretty quickly and soon they are in three groups of three. Three are left to watch. I find it very useful to take actors out of the action and let them watch what is taking place—let them add to and share my movement director's eye. These extra pairs of eyes see all kinds of stories in the game that my one pair cannot. It gives them extra edge when they return to the work. They have seen first hand how the space works when everyone onstage is heeding the music that is being created there.

The game goes well and the actors are producing some beautiful work. Now they return to Act II, Scene I of *A Midsummer Night's Dream*.

> 'Remember the game. We have no leaders here, but, Theseus and Hippolyta, in your slow dream-trance, you are leaders. Occasionally take something of Puck's movement, but at your speed. The rest follow as ye will. Feel the invisible strings between you.'

The scene is played with extraordinary delicacy. Puck dominates, of course, but there is a bewitching interplay of human and fairy, reality and dream surrounding him, placing him, if you like. The actors are listening to each other's music so masterfully that a spell is created. John is excited:

> 'Keep everyone onstage! Now let's have the Mechanicals up front, and the rest at the back; you know, present, but not present in the action. Carry on being leaders, Theseus and Hippolyta, and let's see what happens!'

What happens is utterly engrossing because relationships onstage have now become musical relationships where every little movement has authenticity and meaning.

Movement of any kind can be tricky onstage. Too much control and too much design can be as problematical as random, unchoreographed gesture. But director/ choreographer and actors ought to be able to work hand in hand. It is about recognising that the actor, as I have said above, is author of their own movement—and that means every movement. An actor's random movement can often upset or jar a scene; a delayed reaction causes the punchline to flop; an exit or an entrance can add frighteningly little to the atmosphere onstage. There may be many actors onstage—many random movements producing a chaos of bad timing or anodyne acting. Or, conversely, there may be actors acutely aware of the length of their stride, their every tiny movement… actors listening hard to the rhythm of the piece, to each other, highly conscious of where everybody is, exactly, on the stage, conscious that A has speeded up that particular movement tonight, that B is drumming their fingers on the writing desk with less force than last night… etc. These actors *adapt*, so that each performance is coherent yet utterly new.

Visual Spacing

I do believe it is the job of a movement teacher to train actors to have this level of alertness in performance. If this is not fostered, then the actor will have difficulty embracing anything except the familiar.

The *Leading and Following* exercise is a marvellous tool for actors taking charge of their space onstage, but let's go further back to what would help them *before* this game—the place where they just stand on the stage about to begin.

Nine actors are onstage waiting to begin the game.

'Do they look interesting?' I ask the audience.

'Well, not yet, of course.'

'Actors, are you waiting to begin?'

'Yes.'

'What if I don't tell you to begin for three minutes?'

'Then the audience will be very bored.'

'Lawks! We need to go further back.'

Lecoq's Raft

This exercise, or rather game, is a dead simple and brilliant way of getting student actors to feel the consequence, for want of a better term, of their presence in the theatre space.

We mark out a space: four shoes are useful in designating the four corners of a seven-foot-sided square. The square, I explain to the students, is a raft balanced precariously on the point of a cone. I invite two actors to jump onto the raft but to be sure they don't upset it. The two jump on from opposite sides. The balance of the raft remains, but the play is not about safety, or the audience will fall asleep. The actors, A and B, creep round the edges of the raft, gladiator-style. A rushes to the centre but B is quick enough to get to the centre in time to prevent the raft capsizing. A is determined to oust B from the raft and rushes for a corner. B is quick to reach the opposite diagonal. A throws himself flat towards the centre and B mirrors the movement. It's getting slightly tedious so we introduce a third actor, then a fourth, a fifth. As the numbers increase so does the minute concentration: one foot, one inch in the wrong direction can literally rock the boat.

Visual Spacing

Five actors, numbered 1 to 5, have their backs against the far wall of the studio. Two feet in front of them is the back of the stage. Actor 1 steps forward onto the stage and finds a place to 'be', either standing or sitting. Actor 2 considers Actor 1's position in space, and finds a place to 'be' that has a spatial relationship with the first. Actor 3 enters. The choices are more crucial as the numbers onstage increase: the position of a hand or the turn of a head can make all the difference to drawing an audience into the picture, into the game, though as yet none of us know what the game is.

For example: Actor 1 chooses to sit front on to the audience downstage-right. Actor 2 sits downstage-left, but facing left. Actor 3 sits on Actor 1's left, looking at him. I urge Actor 4 to think of the raft exercise, but think about her relationship to the other three. She stands upstage-left gazing at Actor 1 who cannot see her. She has set up a powerful diagonal between herself and Actor 1. Invisible diagonal lines onstage cut through the horizontals, the parallel lines, and set up poles of conflict and attraction. It's a strong picture now. Actor 5 has to think very hard how to add to it as she is the last piece of the tableau. She lies down on her front, bang in the middle of the stage. I ask her to make another choice and she moves a little upstage-right. She then points, rather like someone who does not wish to be caught, at Actor 2 while gazing at Actor 4. Suddenly the stage is charged with electricity. None of us, least of all the actors, know what this story is about, but it seems that Actors 4 and 5 know something about Actors 1 and 2.

We keep working, change the order. Different groups of five. Take the number of actors up to ten, eleven, twelve… The actors' choices produce the basis of their play, and the choices get bolder. There is nothing random or unbalanced about their presence in the space. I make it harder. The line-up now has to face the back wall. They only turn on the moment they enter the stage. Their decisions and choices have to be lightning quick:

> 'Do I need to give the stage more balance? Change the focus? Augment the focus? Hang on, what is the focus? Is there an atmosphere? No, right, so I create one… Hmmm… Five actors dotted about the stage… all look pretty vacant, dreamy… I think I'll anchor them a bit… so… Yes, I'll take centre stage and put my hand out as though to see if it's raining?'

The space is finally charged. Now what?

We do the exercise again—nine actors facing the back wall. Actors 5, 6 and 9 are leaders. When the starting point is established—the stage full, and full of dynamic stillness—we can begin the *Leading and Following* exercise. An artistic springboard has been created by the awareness of relationship in space, and, of course, where there is relationship, there is play.

Every little movement counts. It is easy to talk about the 'simple gesture', 'economy of movement', 'absolute still-ness', but for a bunch of new acting students these things are very difficult. We have talked about the importance of actors becoming authors of their movement within the group they are working in, but so often an actor is unaware how much he or she is moving. I am endeavouring to make the students hear the music of their movement, yet in the simple movement of sitting on a chair, your actor says it is a case of 'plop' onto a chair. They do not notice the ripples of movement that 'plop' creates in terms of the placing of hands on thighs, the slight lifting of the head, the movement of the eyes, and the shifting of the feet. I have worked on balance and spacing, but to go beyond, in this game, to where there are no leaders or followers, but only musicality, means I now have to concentrate on every little movement.

The Butterfly Effect and Musicality of Movement

The 'Butterfly Effect' is encapsulated in chaos theory. It states that the flutter of a butterfly's wing in China could actually affect weather patterns in New York City. The flapping of a single butterfly's wing produces a tiny change in the state of the atmosphere. Over a period of time, what the atmosphere actually does diverges from what it would have done. So, in a month's time, the tornado that was predicted doesn't happen, but another unpredicted hurricane occurs in another part of the States. If you stop to reflect on this idea, and the idea of predictability, it would seem that chaos was inevitable. Yet there is form and there are patterns, and what is exciting is that no two patterns can be exactly the same.

Four actors are on a stage. A shouts at B. B reacts. It is clear that A has upset B and B's reaction of shock-horror is understandable. C sides with B and turns on A. D refuses to get involved, which creates tension in itself. All is a dialogue of word and gesture. What if we take all that away, so reaction, resonance and response are not dependent on language and gesture (and by 'gesture' I mean those movements that are used to underline language). What if we fine-tune the actors to the relationship drama between movement, and movement within the space. The drama, in fact, of the Butterfly Effect: the vibration of one movement by one actor at one side of the stage, causing a departure from the norm in the rhythm of another actor's movement at the other side, without throwing the entire stage into chaos. In terms of visual spacing and what this means, the students can discover that with as many as thirty people onstage, if they are attuned to the vibration caused by each other's movement and understand vibration in terms of musicality, then they have room to play—and be authors of their theatrical space.

In this way, a movement director of thirty actors is less a choreographer, and more a facilitator. I have devised countless pieces of so-called 'physical theatre' with large groups of actors, and am happy to say I have been congratulated on my 'choreography':

> 'So much is going on, Christian—even in the stillness [and I do a lot of stillness], but you see everything.'

It is not choreography that I am proud of, because my choreography has no power above placing them in the space, but enabling the audience to see it all is something I am proud of. This is musicality of movement.

'Crescendo', 'rallentando', 'rests and repeats' are a few musical expressions that equally apply to the moving body. In movement we talk about 'weight' (strength), 'space' (direction), 'time' (duration), terms usually belonging to Laban. 'Counterweight' (resistance to gravity), 'suspension', 'shock and resonance' are terms belonging to Decroux. Students of acting have to learn that when they move onstage there is an art to this movement which has its own technique, which in essence is musical.

We are always told in acting that there is a point to every movement; every movement is a coherent expression of character; there are few movements which have not been provoked by thought; thought is the motor; every movement has its reason.

It is absolutely true that an actor must be clear of their intention in everything they do, but we must, as teachers, not confuse *intention* with a thought process that can be analysed—God forbid! Of course, we all know that there is nothing worse than empty gesture, movement for the sake of movement (hamming or 'sawing' the air). However, an actor might raise their hand to their forehead with such delicacy that you are overwhelmed by the poignancy of the movement. You could see all the pain of the character in that one economic movement. This is truthful acting. It is genius. You ask this great actor what was the thought behind such a move.

'Oh, I dunno. It felt right.'

'Oh.'

That is the right answer: it felt right for the character in the context of the scene. The right note played at the right time. Can you really teach this? Well, yes, I think you can.

After several years teaching at LAMDA I decided to immerse the students in what I call 'musicality of movement'. I wanted to get them away from their thinking bodies, and into their listening bodies, so that their movement would both 'feel right' and look right in the most bizarre situations.

An Exercise Becomes the Show

In the second term of the second year at LAMDA, with the basic principles of musicality under their belts, and bodies that are beginning to articulate coherently in the space, I set the students a movement piece. I choose a theme— 'greetings' in this case—and stand in the centre of my students. I asked them to imagine going to a faraway land and greeting the village elders.

Auto-contact Movements and Musicality

'Close your eyes and give me your movement of greeting.'

A mixture of lowered heads, extended hands and confused grins surround me.

'Picture the scenery, the dignity of the occasion. Make this greeting a whole-body movement.'

The atmosphere changes and the bodies suddenly become interesting.

'Now a movement of farewell—you will probably never see these people again. Don't think about it, just go ahead. This is not our language—it's a new language. Repeat the two movements and go from one to the other slowly, now fast. Good.'

The students move from greeting to farewell and back again.

'Now choose three auto-contact movements and repeat them in sequence, 1,2,3; 1,2,3; 1,2,3.'

An auto-contact movement is what we do all the time: a movement that involves contacting part of ourselves. For example, movement 1 might be the left arm folded across the waist; movement 2, the right hand travels to the forehead; and 3, the right hand now sweeps over the back of the head and both arms come to the side ready to begin again at 1.

'Christian, what about our greetings?'

'Put them on hold. We are doing auto-contact movements.'

'Oh, okay.'

The students are nonplussed. Where is the artistic connection, the thought connection in all this?

Each student creates a sequence of auto-contact movements.

> 'Now experiment with the rhythm as you go from 1 to 2 to 3 and back to 1. Is your first movement a shock, so the next might be a resonance to that shock, and 2 and 3 a whole-body vibration? What relation does 3 have to 2? Can you sing the movements?'

> 'Sing?'

> 'Yep: shupp (1st movement—i.e. Arm to waist—a shock), pom-pom-pom-pom-pom-tic (2nd movement—right arm slowly to forehead and a moment's suspension—tic—on contact of hand to forehead), vrrump, tic, dad-a-dad-a-da-vrrrrump?'

> 'Did I do vrrrrump?'

> 'Yes, you moved your hand fast and busily over your hair then paused in suspension, 'tic', before moving slowly, 'da da da…' to zero, i.e. your starting point.'

The students slowly begin to get it, and extraordinary sounds fill the studio.

> 'Now add in a head rotation—for example, just before the first 'tic', your head rotates left, tic! Now the music is pom, pom, pom, pom, pom, tic-tic ooooh…!'

Meaningless joining-up of inconsequential movement? A movement of a hand to a forehead is an everyday movement—a habit in some cases, a way of moving hair out of the face—but if it is interrupted by a sudden turn of the head, and the hand is poised mid-air, then it is something else. A thought that interrupted the movement? Something outside that disturbed the subject? At this stage it is not important to know. We do not seek to understand music, but to listen to it. The students work on, and we hone each individual piece so that every little movement is accounted for, and the student is not guilty of 'too many notes'. They watch each other.

Jane says, 'John, your piece is about abandonment.'

Phil says, 'No, it's a prelude to suicide.'

Daimon says, 'No, it's just so sad and so beautiful.'

Sarah says, 'Yeah, abandonment by a girlfriend...'

We ask John what it's about.

'God knows. I'm just going pom pom pom di-dum, splot... huff.'

'Huff?'

'Oh, shut up!'

This is why it is mesmerising: the actor is singing inside. ('*Enchanté*': the true meaning of 'enchanted'.)

Now I ask the students to go back to their movements of greeting and farewell. I put them in pairs: As to move between greeting and farewell, and Bs to interrupt that movement by touching their partner on the shoulder at any point on the journey. A has to stop in suspension when touched. Between greeting and farewell there are a thousand movements—places to pause, to lose balance, to move on from. A is caught off guard—every muscle poised to prevent falling.

'Now work on your own. You are to go from greeting to farewell, at one speed, as slowly as possible. Be certain and clear about the journey before you set out. This should take between five and seven minutes.'

I put on some music to help—a slow movement from a Mozart piano concerto perhaps.

This is incredibly concentrated work. We have already met it in the moving of chairs described in Chapter Two: the body's entire musculature is at work, enabling the journey to happen. There is no time for thought, it is impossible to daydream, the body and mind are entirely concentrated. There can be no extraneous movement, no throwaway gestures. The constant shifting of balance between the body parts to maintain the trajectory is all-focusing. A 'marathon' of a different kind and much tougher. To watch this exercise is one of the most beautiful and moving experiences. When the body is fully involved in this way, it moves us, it is emotional. It does not have to be feeling emotions or having emotional thoughts in order to be emotional. The students watch each other.

They are knackered so we break. The next time we meet I ask them to do some joining-up: they are to put the three auto-contact movements together with the movements of greeting and farewell. Within this sequence there must be at least two accelerations, four movements of rotation of any part of the body, a change in level—i.e. going down to floor level at some point—and there must be a displacement—i.e. a moment of travelling across the space. The piece must be no longer than forty-five seconds and must be cyclical—i.e. they can begin again wherever they have finished. They may add in anything else they like in terms of moments of suspension, 'shocks and resonances', but, above all, they must be able to 'sing' their pieces.

*

'Shock and resonance' must not be confused with 'action and reaction'. The quality of a resonance depends entirely on the quality of the shock, which is not the case where a reaction to an action is concerned.

For every shock, there has to be a resonance. The most obvious example is sound, where the striking of a drum creates a resonance that continues beyond the striking itself. Very few sounds have no discernible resonance, and, if they do, they are usually rather unbearable, e.g. the fingernail scraping the blackboard. No one can say exactly when a resonance either starts or stops, simply that it happens as a result of some kind of impulse, be it the beating of a drum, the plucking of a harp string, the dropping of a pebble into a pool (where the ripples are the resonance), or the fallout of stars from a firework exploding in the sky.

I have found it very important for actors to understand shock and resonance in order to assess their own timing in relation to their own movement and the movement of others.

Shock and Resonance

1. I ask a group of actors to move about the space. When I clap my hands they are to do a whole body-movement of shock as though they have just seen a monster. They walk about again and this time I clap twice: a shock on each clap. We build it up to about six shocks and the effect is very much like that of a strobe lighting effect. Fun for a bit, but ultimately slightly unbearable.

2. I now put the actors in pairs, A and B. A performs a shock or couple of shocks. B, standing close to A, without touching or making eye contact, provides the resonance. This must not be a logical response to the shock, i.e. A moving towards A to see what the matter is (that is a reaction). It is a musical response that depends on the vigour of the shock. For example, A might suddenly double up as though having some kind of attack. B registers the quality of the shock and may move their hand slowly towards their chin. It may not reach the chin (as the resonance may have run out before it gets there), but remains suspended while A performs the next shock(s) to which B creates the appropriate resonance. The listening between the pair is crucial: A must know how great or small his shock has been so as to give B the appropriate resonance space and not cut it short.

3. The actors work alone now. They are to make the shocks smaller—e.g. A fast rotation of the head to the right, followed by the resonance: the fingers of one hand slowly move as though to make a fist. Or a fast movement of the forearm to the mouth followed by a fast inclination of the head backwards to look up (two shocks), and then the resonance: just the eyes slowly lowering, etc. The movements become the outward expression of thoughts.

The exercise can be used in countless ways from the actor alone in a room drinking tea, to a Greek chorus that provides a resonance to the action of the protagonists: not a commentary, not a set of reactions, but a musical response that gives space for the events unfolding to be felt.

The study of shock and resonance allows an actor to feel the impact of his or her actions onstage.

The next few sessions are devoted to each student perfecting their piece, and each piece *has* to be perfect: no extraneous movement, every step accounted for, every blink, breath and vibration having its place. Before they perform, I ask each of them to sit on a chair and sing their piece through. Then they perform. Forty-five seconds of silence followed by another forty-five seconds, and then another, and the musicality of the movement keeps us on the edge of our seats. But this is only the beginning!

Now I put two students on the stage.

> 'Each do your piece three times through as though you were alone onstage. You may get very close to each other. Don't avoid it.'

We watch, our eyes moving between the actors. It's hard to concentrate on them both at once. They have something in common—there is a kind of greeting and farewell thing, but they miss each other. We long for a connection between the two.

> 'Now again, but this time be very aware of each other's "music". Listen to it rather than look, and allow yourself to be affected: perhaps the other's "shock" provides a change in your rhythm, or jumps you like a needle on a record to a different place in your piece…'

The students continue. Now there is the beginning of a connection between the two. They are affected, infected by the other's 'music'.

> 'Get very close—make eye contact… Repeat a movement if you feel like it—borrow a movement from the other.'

Suddenly they are both doing the same movement—it is a moment of agreement, a moving suspension—then they are off into their own language again. Coming together, moments of harmony, moments of understanding, and then moments of being thrown back into an idiotic privacy—a private language. The pulses of their movement ricochet between them. It now seems they need each other for their own movement to have sense in the space. They stop. Fifteen minutes have gone by without a sound, but our ears are ringing.

So now they can borrow, follow, repeat each other's movements and tease their own piece, but are always able to return to its original perfection whenever they wish. The original is absolutely solid. Now we introduce a third person, a fourth, a fifth… The listening intensifies, the connections grow, the borrowing and repetition increase. At one point all are doing one of Emma's movements again and again until Jack crashes back into his piece sending infectious waves of speed and momentary chaos over the studio floor. We keep adding more actors, but after about ten, the actors find it too hard—too many choices. They need a conductor or two. We set up four leaders, each with five followers. Six people watch. The followers follow in the sense of being able to borrow from their leader, stopping when the leader stops. We are back in Enrique Pardo's game, but the leaders lead with their pieces and are followed by followers doing their pieces. The leaders are hugely responsible for the space. They know their language. The choice is how to use it.

The Show

I take a risk and decide to perform it, not knowing what 'it' will be. We choose a title to go with our greetings/farewells: *United Nations?* I choose four leaders. The followers are not random selections: some of the pieces 'chime' better with others, and this has to be taken into consideration. We design the space for the opening. This is in the LAMDA theatre. The show is to be part of a programme of movement, dance and fight. I choose two leaders whose movement pieces work particularly well together. They are to open the show. I suggest a midpoint of the show led by Jane, a leader, and an endpoint led by Giles, another leader. That is all.

An actor steps towards another in absolute silence. He does his movement piece once through before her. It is weirdly beautiful. Everyone is still. Another actor steps towards the same girl and does her piece, once, twice. Something clicks and the girl is propelled into her piece with a vivacity that provokes others into theirs. More meetings take place in this way: dialogue, block, misunderstanding—and the stage is rife with private languages; then the followers regroup, dialogue resumes between leaders, translation happening amongst the followers, agreement to differ… It is all there and it all ends with quizzical resolution where twenty-eight actors stand immobile in their individual stances—all different, but all gently tapping their index fingers against their cheeks. The final resonance of a long debate.

The show lasted thirty minutes in complete silence.

'Marvellous choreography, Christian. The visual spacing was extraordinary! How did you do it?'

I truthfully replied that I did not know what was going to happen for most of the show.

'Then how…?'

I only know I taught them the power of musicality of movement, and I am very proud of it. Having devoted time and a performance to this seemingly very abstract discipline, the dividends were enormous. Afterwards, I asked the students what they felt motivated the show. They looked puzzled and then answered in one.

'Well, we had very good things we wanted to say—in movement, of course—but we had to listen in order to say it!'

'Working like this, movement seems bigger than thinking. It makes the story happen before your head does.'

I worked with the same group the following summer. We were devising a show, using text, creating scenarios. The students worked tirelessly with minute attention to detail. They knew exactly how near and how far apart they should be from one another at any given time. This sounds banal and uncreative, but it is exactly the opposite: by having an inherent understanding of the power and importance of the musicality of their own movement within a given context, they could feel the invisible connections between each other—the tiny movement of one actor affecting the atmosphere of the whole, infecting the atmosphere, changing it unpredictably, touching it unpredictably but truthfully, within the context. The vibration of the butterfly's wing.

Most actors have a good sense of rhythm and timing, and small theatre companies, especially those that improvise a great deal, learn how to work the stage musically. Yet how often, when large casts are involved, does this musicality stuff get ignored or handed over to a choreographer for some 'movement bits'? A movement director is there to alert the cast to the potential of its musicality, its power to listen and be heard. When that is done, a director's vision becomes a greater reality than he or she could ever have dreamed of.

Chapter Ten

The Mystery of Music and Props

The Role of Music

Music can be, and usually is, a powerful presence onstage that deserves careful respect. I love working with music, and it holds a crucial if not essential place in my work with actors. In the simplest terms, music energises and invigorates—what better way to get going after lunch in an all-day rehearsal than with Scottish dance-band music and fifteen minutes of quickstep? Music offers a new dimension, an atmosphere. Let's face it, there doesn't exist a culture where music is not there, if not to take us beyond, then at least to dance...

And this is why the actor must beware. Decroux said, 'How can the muscle used for work, which moves because it has to, be the same muscle used in dance which moves because it wants to?' The actor, for me, has to be utterly aware of their movement. Each movement is something that comes from the heart of the character. Economy of movement, unity of mind and body in movement is paramount. In class or rehearsal, music provides another voice, a voice that needs listening to as much as you would a fellow actor, but not one to be seduced by. The actor must understand this to give music its proper theatrical space.

Often I have fed music into an impro with the strict instruction to listen to the music—i.e. to work with it as opposed to move to it. All too often the actors let the music dictate, and then the movement follows the music. The work becomes at best bland, and at worst, the movement turns into symmetrical gestures reminiscent of an Eastern bloc parade, and perspective becomes slave to a good rousing tune. If actors were trained dancers, this might be bearable, but the point is that they are not.

In performance and rehearsal I use music as a mysterious fellow actor which provides colour, emotion and a new dimension.

Actors and Objects

During the time I taught at LAMDA, I would often throw in about fifteen minutes of improvisation at the end of a session—seemingly irrelevant to the material we had been concentrating on. Nothing unusual about that. One of these impros became something of a necessary favourite of mine.

Sitting the students facing the impro space, I said, 'The title of this improvisation is *Enter the Stage and Sit on a Chair.*' I placed a chair in the middle of the space. There was usually an eager queue for this clearly straightforward impro. Jack entered, upstage-right, eyes fixed on the chair, marched towards it, sat down and then lifted his head to meet my gaze with a look of triumph.

'Next!'

Brendon decides to vary Jack's approach by running in. He plonks himself on the chair.

'Next!'

We endure about ten variations on Jack's entry, and all the impros have lasted between seven and ten seconds. I look at the rest of the group. They each have the look of someone about to have a medical. I gently ask them if they are having a nice and interesting time and they look nonplussed.

'Aren't you?' asks Jack, boldly.

Very truthfully, I say I am bored rigid. Naturally they are a bit shocked.

> 'Listen: the title of the impro is *Enter the Stage and Sit on a Chair*. That is the title. Dickens wrote a book called *Hard Times*. It had a bit more to it than a paragraph about someone having a hard time.'

> 'Oh, so you want a story?'

> 'I want an impro entitled *Enter the Stage and Sit on a Chair*. At the moment I get the peculiar feeling that there are invisible, giant magnets on the chair that inexorably draw each of you to it as soon as you step into the space. Is that it? Whenever we come across a chair do we make a silent resolution, "It must be sat on, now"?'

I suddenly remember the priceless expression Decroux used to describe a way of standing, swayed back, with the bottom sticking out: '*La nostalgie pour la chaise…*' which conveys 'the yearning for the chair'.

'Oh, I get it,' I hear whispered behind me, and Alec gets up. With tremendous energy he rushes about the stage, exhausted, panting, and desperate to rest. We have several minutes of this powerful activity, and then, eureka! He spots the chair and sits down. End of impro.

> 'So you were worn out, but didn't spot the chair for two minutes. How was that?' I ask, perplexed by this awful impro.

Alec is duly crestfallen.

'What is the chair?' I ask, uncomfortably, feeling the question comes from some kind of diabolical 1970s theatre experiment.

'Well, it's just a chair. Any old chair,' puts in Jack, hopefully.

'Well, that is exactly the point. It is not just a chair. It's the chair of the impro.'

'You mean we must decide what kind of chair it is?'

Impro classes can get like this and if you don't believe me, read Keith Johnstone's marvellous books on the subject.

'No, not beforehand, this is an impro.'

We all sit down and talk.

'A chair is an artefact that has a thousand uses. It is your desk chair, the nursing chair, your comfy armchair, it is the chair you sit on when you've been naughty, it is the chair you stand on to reach the box of chocolates, it is the mouse's hiding place, the child's den, it is a throne… I could go on and on. The point is, it is anything you want it to be, and it is onstage with you. It is your fellow actor. If drama happens as a result of relationship, which it usually does, then relationship is important. Relationship is not just something that happens between people. In this impro you are not alone onstage; there is a chair, and because of the impro's title, there is a relationship with the chair that is sharing your space.'

Margaret stands up. She enters the space open, ready, no baggage. She glances at the chair and then is lost in thought for a moment. She looks stage-right as though she has heard something and then ponders for a while. She passes the chair and glances at it again. Her hand passes through her hair several times, pauses mid-air. Has she thought of something? She laughs to herself and stands behind the chair, letting her right hand fall… Just before it hits the back of the chair it stops in suspension and then lowers itself to contact the hard wood, caressing it while she gazes long and hard at the seat, lost in thought. In this mood she crouches by the chair, hugging it to her. She is beautiful with the chair, eminently watchable. What is the story? No idea, but the musicality of what she is doing invites us into this world where exists only herself and the chair. We are glued. The camera is on her and the chair. With a sudden movement, she seems to shake herself, she stands up, and is clearly about to sit down on the chair, but just before her bottom touches the seat she exits at a run and returns with a book. Her left hand is on the back of the chair. Now, surely, she will sit down. Nope, she picks up the chair and moves it a little stage-left, and then sits down.

'What was going on?' asks a fellow student.

'I was playing at being with the chair—and well, it was *my* chair,' says Margaret.

I mention this exercise because although props, costume and furniture are an obvious quantity in the actor's world, there can be—especially for the inexperienced actor—a sense that these things are crutches rather than properties. Actors can lean on their props, or conversely, be careless with them. When these two things happen, the prop is denied the value of its presence onstage, and so the relationship between actor and object does not exist and certainly cannot develop. Margaret's impro worked, not because she was madly focusing on the chair, but because she was bringing it into her orbit in a way that was musical and inviting. As a result she became very watchable. We began to be in suspense about when she was going to sit down!

Decroux had a marvellous phrase: '*frôler contre le quotidienne*', which literally means, 'to brush, in passing, the everyday'. By this he meant that the actor should go close to what we expect a person in a given situation to do (e.g., holding a glass of wine and lifting it to the lips), but arrest our expectation (of drinking the wine, by turning the head to look out of the window). The play of drinking from the wine glass not only informs us about the actor, but keeps us in suspense. This is exactly what Margaret had done.

The objects we surround ourselves with are, to different extents, emotive; conjuring up people, memories, feelings. They have meaning attached to them and can take us somewhere else. This is pretty much true of any object in the home, and though, surely, your old cutlery cannot be 'emotive' as such, you will use it with a natural familiarity or disgust that your visitors will not, not so much because they are visitors as because the cutlery is your property.

Nowhere is the power of objects more keenly felt than in the theatre and on film. Poisoned chalice, dagger, gun, ring, boot, faded rose… the list is endless. These objects are in the play for a reason. We, the audience, are drawn to them through their handling in the show, and through them we are transported to a new chapter in the evolution of the play. A director can gauge the growing power of, say, the poisoned chalice, by certain decisions: where to place it, how to handle it, the build-up before its appearance, etc. Sometimes the build-up is not given enough time or is overextravagant, thereby not giving the object's appearance the significance that it is due.

The sooner the actors can get their hands on props in the rehearsal process, the better. Objects need to be tried, tested and played with.

Mask

Student actors must not be careless with props, but both respect them and give them time if the props in question are going to enhance their own performance. Neutral mask work is very helpful here: the neutral-mask wearer opens his or her eyes and sees an empty space with an object in it that they have never seen before (a boot, for example). Childlike, the eyes of the mask are drawn towards the object, towards its strangeness, its shiny toe, the little holes for the laces, the noise it makes when you beat the heel on the ground. Perhaps the mask gets angry with the boot and discards it, or turns it into a hat, tying the laces under the chin, or cradling it... The point is that as the relationship between mask and object grows, a rhythm of sorts develops, which changes the nature of the space. The dimensions of the space change in this new relationship. This is something the actor must be aware of when handling objects: it is not just about actor and object, but actor, object and the space they are in. Objects and people change space, and space changes objects and people.

To grasp this in its simplest form, I often get actors to feel the difference on their mode of being and on their voice in walking, on their own, then with a partner and then with a prop, under the stars on a frosty night, walking into the low-ceilinged, crowded office for the Christmas party, and walking down the nave at Chartres Cathedral. In each instance there is architectural rhythm—the rhythm that exists as a result of being in a particular space. Where the example of the mask is concerned, the boot didn't invite the mask into a new space, but the mask's play with the boot did; a new toy can take a child into a new play zone because of the relationship that develops, not because of the toy per se. This is all very obvious, yet inexperienced actors often fail to get this relationship, and to realise it is a relationship through, and as a result of, *play.*

Now, take the kind of scenario where the actor is required to hurl plates on the floor and stomp on them in rage. The character is in a state of abject hysteria and high tension. Not the actor: the actor is playing the rage and the breaking of plates can become something extraordinary. But sometimes improvising actors like to throw props about a bit. The director/teacher can easily spot the fine line between 'play' and 'not play' here. The audience forget the 'play' when they start worrying about the nice varnished floor and the steel-legged chair being tossed about on it. This was not the actor's intention. Actors are rarely playing when things get dangerous like this.

Spending time with props, and the exact props that are to be used in the show (not any old substitutes) gives an actor the chance to discover how their character holds a knife and fork, how they wind a watch… etc., and as the exploration grows, the character grows, and so their influence on the space, and its influence on the actor, changes.

The Key, the Duck and the Hankie

Working on a show with LAMDA's students in the first year of their three-year acting course, I was troubled how, when I assigned props to a number of students, these objects were left on the studio floor overnight, sat on by mistake, and in some cases, broken. They had no more value, it seemed, than discarded sweatshirts.

I didn't say anything, but next day I gathered the students together in a close circle. From a bag, I carefully placed on the floor in front of them a group of miscellaneous objects: a little rubber duck, a hankie, a heavy beaded plastic necklace, a bent spoon, a small pocketbook, a postcard, a Yale key on a ribbon, an empty Coke can and a little plastic horse. I said I would like one of them to choose an object, and taking it in their hands, to see what happened.

Jo was first. She rummaged—pushing the objects this way and that, and grabbed the necklace. She immediately put it on, clucking nervously when she couldn't fix the fastening. Jo is a talented actor.

Gary was next. Following Jo's example, he too rummaged, though a little more businesslike, took the postcard, put it in front of him and gazed at it for a minute. 'I've finished,' he said, looking up. He too is a talented actor.

What was the matter? Why was this bunch so unresponsive to my collection, why so boorish, why so self-limiting? I couldn't bear any more so I stopped them, gently.

'Jo, what did the necklace feel like?'

I didn't want her to say 'gems' or 'diamonds', but I wanted to see if she had actually *felt* the necklace.

'Oh, I don't know.' She felt it. 'Plastic.'

'Right. Put the objects back in the centre, and all of you close your eyes. Each object is something none of you have seen before. You may have seen a small rubber duck, but you haven't seen this one before. It is my special collection, so therefore precious—in fact, worth a great deal. They have value, these things, because each object takes me into a different time, a different place, a different way of being. Now really look at them.'

The group open their eyes.

Piers gently reaches out his hand. He knows exactly what he wants to pick up—the Yale key. Without disturbing the other props, he carefully lifts the key and feels its serrated blade—as though running a finger over the teeth of a comb. His body is absorbed in his 'looking', fully focused on this small object. All eyes are drawn to the key. The key is on a ribbon, and Piers lets it swing on a finger before laying it on his knee. He sits, immobile—the tension is growing, and he turns it with the tip of his finger. The tension increases, ostensibly nothing much is happening, yet a huge amount is happening.

Piers' whole-body intent is wrapped up with an object we know as a 'key'. As a result, we are drawn towards Piers and his key. We cannot stop watching him. (In a doctor's waiting room full of people shifting in their chairs, coughing, looking at their watches, etc., it is the boy intent on opening and closing the blades of his penknife that we recall...)

Piers finishes. 'Was that bearable?' I ask.

'God, Christian. "Bearable"! It was amazing. He could have gone on and on.'

'Piers, what was going on!'

'Oh, I just realised what an extraordinary object a Yale key is.'

Now the students each take an object into a private place. The students left over sit and watch. I quietly ask one of them to discreetly video what is going on.

Once the actor is 'with' the object, and their intent is on the object, the atmosphere changes and draws us in. This does not happen so much when the actor *decides* to 'do' something with the object, or lets it fulfil its prescribed purpose, as in the putting on of the necklace. But with intent, relationship is created, and this comes across very clearly on the video. Where the actor has a relationship with a prop and is cultivating that relationship and even rejecting it, there is drama. The times the actor felt they *had* to do something *without* the body's engagement, the video showed bland, empty and uninteresting footage.

We finish the exercise and go back to rehearsing the play in hand, gathering the appropriate props. The rehearsal is transformed. A 'servant' has to place a necklace around her mistress's neck. The actor now has a sense of the necklace's place onstage: the necklace of her queen; a thing of value and great workmanship. Her concentration at this moment draws us to her utter devotion to the queen, apparent, not in the text as this servant has few lines, but in the simple action with the necklace.

Much of this working with props is so simple, so obvious, but unless students have had time with their props, have been encouraged to understand that these objects share the space, and in some sense are fellow actors with influence, there is little point in them! I would urge any director to get hold of the play's props as early as possible in rehearsal, and try not to do with substitutes as far as they can. Actors need to find their props' properties.

Chapter Eleven

Pastoral Care

Teaching and training naturally carry with them an amount of pastoral care, and where the teaching of movement is concerned, perhaps more so.

Our bodies store events in a far more complex way than do our minds or our so-called 'memories'... birthdays, celebrations, picnics, seaside fun, accidents, moments of panic... but these tend to be incidents. The body's memory is far more comprehensive. A trauma where the body is concerned is not simply a 'bad time': it is a process where muscles contract to protect the body, and adrenaline is pumped around it in a fight or flight response. The body's chemistry is changed. The vibration, the imprint of the trauma is retained in the body. One of the effects of relaxation is to unlock the muscles that hold these vibrations, and this can be manifested in weeping, gasping, even screaming. Of course, it is not only pain that is released, but giggling, euphoria, deep happiness, and the feeling of being in love, which are all, equally, stored in the body.

The body can rarely hide trauma, illness, depression, anxiety, drug-addiction, eating disorders... The signs are picked up fairly speedily at any point in the training. A simple relaxation exercise can unleash powerful emotions. The space has to be safe, and the students have to be enough of a group to be held in this space. This is a teacher's responsibility.

In many respects, an actor's training involves bringing people to an edge in order that they may fly in new and undiscovered directions. It can be a dangerous journey and teachers and directors of students must be very careful of what they are doing. Every student will react differently under pressure, and a kick up the backside might be appropriate for one, so to speak, but wreck another. Generalised pushing to the edge and forcing students to open up (a method in some drama schools) is usually counterproductive and dangerous. We all know about the danger of 'vacuums', and if a barrier is broken, something must be put in its place. Exercises plucked at random to probe and open up without due regard for the individual and that individual's position in the group are not acceptable.

The demands of training can mean times of particular strain. It is important that a group can hold individuals at these times, but the group cannot be expected to carry difficult situations indefinitely. Holding a person and delving into a person's issues, health or otherwise, are two different processes and each has their appropriate time and space. The teacher must make the distinction.

My colleagues and I like to stress to students that the studio space is not only a working space, it is a free and neutral space where problems and personal baggage are left outside. Not a place to hide, but a place to be free of distraction. Easy to say; less easy if you are an eighteen-year-old in serious need of help.

LAMDA now employs a counsellor/psychotherapist, and I feel all such institutions should have a similar resource. Teachers cannot and should not play the role of therapist. We have neither the time nor the tools. Neither do fellow students.

A Note About Typecasting

If it appears that a particular student is ideal for a particular role, then one must ask exactly what about them is 'ideal'. Are they ideal because at this moment of their training it would be ideal for them to have the challenge that this role presents, or they are ideal because they fit the ideal vision the director has of that character (ideal in professional theatre, but not necessarily ideal nor necessarily appropriate where students are concerned)? If the latter is the case, then one must ask directors to remember these actors are students. If the director does not know the students prior to casting, then he or she needs to be primed as to the student's needs at this point of their training. However, this rarely happens.

As a visiting movement director in a number of drama schools outside LAMDA, I've often been told, 'Oh, you'll like so and so in your show', or 'Anna is so good at movement, but don't give her a speaking part: hopeless in the voice department...' Anna was a marvellous Italian student. She moved beautifully, but English not being her first language, she found text difficult. 'Let's face it, she won't get work over here.' Then why had she been accepted into this particular drama school? She was at the end of her first year and we were about to do *Antigone*. I cast her as Antigone—a huge speaking role. She was an excellent actor and badly needed this challenge. Extra hours were put in with the voice coach and she produced a performance that was worthy of any of Peter Brook's actors. Her first job after leaving college was with the Royal Shakespeare Company.

Chapter Twelve

Working with Children

Schoolchildren and Space

When I first started working with adults I would come home on a high, and busily start recording the day's events and planning the next class. When I first started working with children I would come home and go to bed. On the whole this hasn't changed much.

Taking theatre and storytelling into schools is a very different business from the ongoing teaching of drama students, or from the one-off workshops in colleges or for adult Joe Public—but what connects them is, of course, play. Students accept you as an integral part of their training; adults tend to sign up for your course; children don't. If you are a one-off in an established curriculum you have a day in which to add something fresh, a new diversion to their ongoing study. To be efficient, to be successful, to have served its purpose, the one-off has to be an event. Where this is so, under the teacher's hat lurks the brightly coloured performer's cap.

In all teaching there is performing. Every teacher would agree, I think. I would be lying if I said my teaching is all about the selfless imparting of information and technique. No. A sizeable amount is plain showing-off, and I love it. So do the students, as a rule. It is important to show off a little. It is your right. You are the expert here. No little girl wants to do ballet with a teacher who doesn't play the part of ballet dancer to some extent. Demonstrating your skill, past or present, is part of the package. Now, when it comes to working with children, performing means something slightly different. It means being ready to change character many times, yet be relentlessly yourself.

Whatever project I am doing at any particular time in a primary school, I keep asking myself, not 'What is drama in schools for?', but 'What do I want the children to go away with?' Many small children, if you ask them the intolerable question, 'What did you do today?' will often reply, 'I can't remember', or change the subject. If something has really made an impression, they will, usually, tell you sooner or later.

In my blurb for schools I talk about 'citizenship'. 'Citizenship' was the buzzword at the beginning of this century, and is now part of the National Curriculum. The idea behind 'citizenship' is to give pupils the knowledge, skills and understanding they need to lead confident, healthy, independent lives, and to become informed, responsible citizens.

My workshops are called 'Drama and Citizenship'. Basically, you cannot be a good actor, or indeed even get a play off the ground, unless you are a good 'citizen' in this sense. Drama and physical theatre have to be shared experiences. One actor cannot try to be a 'better' actor than another. The process is a company one in which the interdependency of the actors is crucial to the quality of the work... The actor learns to take responsibility for him or herself... And it is this responsibility that gives the student independence in a totally interdependent situation.

This seems a little over-the-top when we are talking about four- and five-year-olds, but if we change the word 'actor' and use 'player' instead, then we are playing an enormous game for which there are rules. The player has to take turns, respect their fellow players, and listen to instructions, in order for the play to work, in order to be in play. This last is the nub of the work, and why drama in schools is so important. In the 'play' it is the children's chance, perhaps their only chance, to be something or someone else—to inhabit a character or an atmosphere utterly different from their own. You might say this happens all the time in the simple act of a child's playing, and to an extent that is right. However, children's games happen in friendship groups, many do no imaginary play, and the time when they can, ie. in unsupervised time, is becoming more and more limited. Thus, allowing children to become 'players' is very, very important.

Playing a role can stretch a child. Young children are usually very quick to enter a role and will be in it one hundred per cent. Being 'in it' is actually where they would like to remain. Yes, the unfolding of the story is exciting and brings in many new players, rules of the game and structure, but given half a chance, your four- and five-year-olds would happily stay as elves in a mountain, worms in the earth or giants crossing continents for the whole session. The end product is important, but being in the work is much more important, because it is in those spaces of 'being something else' that a child grows: their entire body indulges in a new physicality, a new shape, a new world. It has to reach out.

Perhaps a child's first bid for 'self-dom' is a bid for space. It is birth. There is simply not enough space to move comfortably any more inside the womb. Drastic action is needed. Drastic action is birth, and the baby now has the appropriate space for the next stage of its development. For the baby it is now a constant testing and pushing of boundaries, reaching, grabbing, throwing, pulling, tantrums, first steps, running, running away... And in this ongoing bid for space, the child is protected by the parents' setting of boundaries, defining the space, i.e. bedtime routines, regular meals, nap times, etc. Without these definitions, space can be overwhelming.

Unstructured Time

In her private play, my daughter's state is one of being in action. Not unlike the actor, she is thoroughly in her role, but her world has no need of the actor's awareness that takes in an audience. Her play is a very serious, private business inhabiting a separate space, one to which I am not privy. It is a crucial space, as crucial as the process of digestion.

'Digestion' is a key word here. To digest food, events, stresses, the day's work, adults often require a different space. 'I'm off to the gym to work off the day', 'I need to rest', 'I'm going to meditate for half an hour', etc. There is a conscious change of space to digest the previous activity. Without these changes of space, an adult can become ill. 'Let's sit down and have a cup of tea' often prevents a fuse blowing. Children's 'digestion' in this sense is less consciously defined, but all the more important. The spaces between activities designed by adults (and these can include organised playtimes with other children) are important digestion moments: here an adult might need a period of inaction following high energy or a high-stress activity, but a child needs to be 'in action' in a different activity. A child hauled away from a playmate for bathtime may spend fifteen minutes on the loo talking or singing to themselves: this is a digestion moment, a space between. A child asks to go and play after a Sunday lunch. The adults are tediously sitting at the table. Of course the child is bored by the adult space, but also their body is craving the space to follow its

thought processes before the next adult-imposed activity—
e.g. the afternoon walk. The child needs to play in the space
between these activities, or, rather, must create space
between them.

This is a time for digestion for the child, and so a time for
growth, a time for processing, and all three contribute to a
stronger sense of 'self'. Why 'self'? Because in play, in these
spaces between adult-orientated activity (though of course
it is labelled 'child-orientated'), the physical, mental and
emotional are inextricably linked in a timeless activity. This
takes place within the boundaries of a safe space, thereby
allowing the child to enter a 'new' space. In this new space,
the child has authority.

✳

I often used to make the mistake of feeling I needed to have
more energy than the children: I would workshop
'tremendously'; 'never a dull moment' sort of thing. It
comes from an idea, manifest amongst children's TV
presenters, that silence and space are dangerous things that
should be avoided at all costs. Like a car going at one
hundred miles an hour, the passengers might get to where
they wish quicker, but they will not have seen much along
the way.

Fidgeting and behavioural problems rarely manifest
themselves where there is space or silence. They become
apparent when I try to get through all that I have prepared.
They are often, in themselves and by their nature, a cry for
space—a cry to be altogether elsewhere.

Too many choices, too few boundaries, and space is
frightening. It cannot be perceived as freedom if one's
starting point isn't security. It can remove our definition of
ourselves by simply being indefinite. One might call it the
abyss.

Back to the Floor

So, with my groups in primary schools, I start quietly—often on the floor. Name games, name rhythms. 'I'm Jack and I like sausages…' Every child is heard in the opening circle. If they are a little older (seven to nine) we 'change' the world. 'I'm Emma and I come to school in a rolled-up newspaper!' Round the group we go. If anyone can't think of something, we leave them and come back to them at the end. Gradually the suggestions become more and more extraordinary ('I come to school in an elephant's ear!'), and unspoken permission is given to play, be weird, but give space to others. We talk about what theatre is, what mime is, what a good audience is, what a bad audience is, and how horrid that is. Ground rules for supportive behaviour are being laid down. We do some character work, we do paired work, we get on the floor. This last is especially important as the boys can't wait to wriggle across large spaces.

All exercises are based on things that appear in the story I will tell later. An exercise is never an exercise only, it is a mime story, a game, a play. So it is with my adult students. A physical exercise that my acting students have difficulty with, becomes very possible when I turn it into a little play: the body accepts play far better than coercion, however 'good for you' it is packaged. The body is listening, energy follows thought. The body literally 'performs' the exercise. Many of the problems that arise from aerobics classes in terms of sprains, strains, and only short-term fitness, are due to the fact that they are 'got through', rather than performed.

The children do some mime. I mime a boomerang. What is clever about a boomerang? I am going to throw 'it' around the circle of children at shoulder height. Can they duck in time? There's always some smart alec who won't duck, and has some witty explanation or does a dramatic death. Okay, we all do dramatic deaths. What about the boomerang? We talk about stealing the show, spoiling the illusion. Smart alec is embarrassed, but his 'death' was very funny.

I perform some very bad mime and ask them to spot the mistakes. The focus is always on listening, observing, working together. The focus would be the same if they were grown-ups, but there the skill of the teacher is about letting the adults find the freedom to feel and discover, whereas with children it is about giving them the security to have freedom. Security in the group. Solid boundaries.

Now there is the story. In my work in primary schools, every group has a story. By now about a third or even half my allotted time will have passed. With the tiny ones I do the story with them as I tell it. From about Year Two upwards (six- to eight-year-olds) we sit again, and I tell the story. Now I go for it. I must know this story inside out and back to front, because it might well have to change suddenly, depending on the needs of the group. My story is a performance full of colour, character, repetition, sound effects and pregnant pauses. I am master of my story and I love it. Sometimes the story can take a good twenty minutes to tell, and if I tell it well there are no interruptions, no disruption and I find myself asking, 'What is ADHD?' Of course I do not for one moment deny its existence, and I've had some horrendous times with impossible children, but *never* at storytime. This time is precious and I must get it right—be absolutely sure of my materials—be utterly present—act, in fact!

It's a question of time management. If there is time we do the whole story, or if not we might take three parts of it—the beginning, middle and end (deciding what these are is good material for debate)—work in groups, work on a soundscape, let the children become the props, the scenery, the monsters, the dragons, and work to find new endings…

Whilst doing the story, repetition is essential. For an adult, technique requires repetition. It makes perfect sense that the French word for 'practice' is '*répétition*'. Practice gives strength and security in technique. For children, repetition is like a glorious signal to redo what they have got used to, what they have enjoyed, be it chanting, singing, skipping— part of a scene… again and again. (*Teletubbies* have totally grasped this.) Repetition provides a focal point, a 'return' to your places' point, and can focus thirty to forty kids very quickly. Witness Paul.

Paul was a small boy in Year Two in a primary school in Swanage. He had severe Attention-deficit Hyperactivity Disorder (ADHD), and a teaching assistant would be at his side all the time to restrain his outbursts of violent activity. He would throw himself to the floor with frightening violence and was unable to keep concentrated at any level. We were doing a story about the later adventures of Jack (and his beanstalk). We began by 'doing' Jack's mother's kitchen: one child was the fridge (he could cleverly 'light up' when his 'door' was opened), another was the old saucepan, another the old stew in the old saucepan, another a box of cornflakes, another the only cornflake left… So it went on. Suddenly, Paul shouted, 'I'll be a crumb.' So he curled up and was a perfect, absolutely still crumb for seven minutes. We returned to this scene two more times, and the perfect positioning of his crumb became more and more splendid. The ADHD was on hold. He was an actor with a vital role. Repetition here made him the actor essential to this scene.

The lovely thing about doing drama with children is that your material has probably provoked hundreds of stories and ideas you could never possibly have imagined. Also, you can enjoy what you love: performing. Slipping in and out of role enables you to bring a group back together, enables you to get their attention, enables them to be carried away (often drastically) into a new world of adventure and strangeness. If they get too excited I never shout. It tends to wear me out. I might leave the room for a moment, or use a drum to bring them back. Yet the slipping in and out of character can be very tiring. It is an easy mistake to start 'entertaining'. That is why returning to the floor, being quiet, is crucial. You may have another and more complicated group of thirty children coming in in a few minutes. Budgets, timetables, etc. are very hard to work round, but if you are going to make a habit of children's drama workshops, I would suggest never doing more than four hours on any given day. The energy used in these workshops is far greater than the routine of class teaching. This must be recognised if only by you, and it was only by getting thoroughly worn down that I realised it too.

Nowadays, I try to end all my children's workshops on the floor, with all the eyes closed. I use music and take them on a guided fantasy, a gentle trip, if you like. We only ever do this at the end of the workshop. They curl up comfortably, not too near one another and imagine they are flying, riding a pony, being a tiny kitten… they travel. The imagination is happy to fly and the bodies relax and become calm. At the end they are ready to move on to their next class. There will always be some who cannot do this: their bodies contain too much adrenaline, but the calmed atmosphere of the others will affect them, if only a little. Return the children to their teacher *having* entered a different space, not still in the middle of the drama!

Chapter Thirteen

Working with the Army

It is a good idea to be in Yellow Pages. An old friend and colleague, Roland Allen, registered his excellent Theatre in Education (TIE) company, Big Wheel, under 'D' for Drama, and that is where captains Lisa and Jane spotted him from their desks at the Army School of Education at Worthy Down, near Winchester. 'This is your sort of thing, Christian,' said Roland and gave them my number.

'We need some drama for our POD course.' Very friendly.

'POD?'

'Potential Officer Development. It's a fourteen-week course for men who want to get into Sandhurst and become officers.'

'What had you in mind?'

'Well, you know, drama. They are going to the theatre next week!'

I agreed to do a day's 'drama' with the twenty or so 'Potential Officers'. This turned out to be a fixture three times a year for the next six years.

The POD course has something of the finishing school about it. The POs are learning what it takes to be an officer, and this varies from having good history lessons on the world wars, to learning how to dress correctly for cocktail parties. Somehow I felt that drama would be closer to the latter activity if I was not careful. (The young soldier who met my train on that first workshop giggled, and asked me if they would all have to be 'trees'.)

Clearly I had carte blanche to do what I liked. I'd made it clear that the work was movement-based and they were to be dressed appropriately. I'd brainstormed my friends to glean any nuggets of useful information concerning the army, but kept returning to the clichéd images of uncomfortable boots, shaven heads and the gnawing question, 'Well, who does join the army these days?' This was at the time of continuing IRA violence and the Bosnian conflict full on.

I sat down and thought in my inexperienced way about the qualities of a good officer: leadership, clarity of communication, appropriate sensitivity, alertness... The list continued. Basically, not dissimilar to the qualities cultivated in an actor's training. I decided to explore boldly the difference between listening and obeying. Surely this was something the future officer should consider?

That first workshop they were very courteous, called me 'Mum' which was slightly disconcerting, and giggled helplessly when asked to do anything. I was female, smallish, billed to do 'drama' in a thoroughly male environment, despite the two captains Lisa and Jane and two of their own number who were beautiful, elegant girls.

I broke the ice by talking their language, the language of physical stamina. I put them through a gruelling warm-up. No complaints. They sweated profusely, but executed my instructions to the T. I was no drama wimp.

We moved on to a variety of simple awareness exercises. Now they had to listen to themselves, feel what was happening. They struggled. Obeying an order has a clear directive. Here there was no clear goal so there was immediate resistance: 'I can't feel anything and I don't see the point.' How judgement blocks listening! But I was in no position to judge: after all, a soldier who gets all touchy-feely and can talk about it is maybe not an efficient soldier. But a soldier whose body is alert is surely an efficient soldier? As the time went on I changed and modified the exercises until everyone had felt a change in their body to some degree. It was challenging for me and frightening for them, but it was an area of work we kept returning to, allowing them to notice changes.

Moving on to listening and observing each other developed the idea of how much you can be trained to notice. I put the soldiers in pairs, A and B. A would watch B play *Grandmother's Footsteps*. Afterwards, A gave B a five-minute commentary of exactly how B moved, what tactics he used, and whether he enjoyed the game or not.

Grandmother's Footsteps (see Chapter Five) is the most marvellous of games that becomes a riot with even the shyest of players. The POs are playing, their bodies all equally alert, and the hidden hierarchy in the group is temporarily forgotten. They are now much more receptive and I can go on pushing, gently.

The Bamboo Poles

I get out my bamboo poles. Four-foot six-inch poles balanced horizontally between partners on the middle finger of each of their right hands (if they're right-handed). This is an exercise adapted from Monika Pagneux's invaluable work, and is as magical in its effect as it is fun. For me, the teacher, the exercise allows me to really see my student. Its effect is akin to turning on a light and saying, 'That's how the room really is', only here the 'room' is a Potential Officer.

I stress there are very important rules to the game. Number one, like in the *'I Throw You the Ball'* game, it must be their favourite game, and number two, they play it with their best friend (more sniggering and plenty of teenage behaviour: 'Yuk, I'm not his best friend'). The idea is to make your partner drop the pole, but remain 'best friends'. The game is light and fun. So far no one is poked in the eye. We watch a few: when the game is *played*, it is safe and the partners enjoy dazzling us with athletic tricks. When one of them wants to 'win', it become dangerous and heavy. We, the audience, stop enjoying the game; our only concern is that they don't get hurt. So 'winning', not 'listening', limits technique, is absolutely no fun, and horrible to watch!

Next I ask them to move the pole, eyes closed. This time the pole must not drop. Many try and go at the same speed as before. The poles clatter to the floor.

One couple is moving very slowly: it is a dance. The bodies are very vulnerable, listening. It is somewhat unnerving for the others and there are a few catcalls. The couple continue and do not drop the pole. Every part of their bodies is listening. The POs understand, and when the couple finish they receive a round of applause.

We move straight on. Too many questions, too much discussion at this stage will only block the listening we are trying to achieve. Now the hard part: again the pole must never drop, but this time one of the pair is leader, is in charge, leads the other. The other, naturally, follows. I point out that one person of the pair will usually feel more comfortable either leading or following. Oh, were it as simple as that, yet it is a fascinating and revealing process they are now embarked on. The point is to have the possibility of enjoying both leading and following. After all, this is still their favourite game.

I watch every couple. Every couple is watched by all. PO Jameson appears not to be able to lead tiny, wiry PO McPherson. Has Jameson no leadership skills? Is it that simple? He is a big man and is not having a good time. Each time he makes a deliberate 'gesture of leadership' McPherson seems to back off, and Jameson has to catch him up in order that the pole does not fall. In fact he is following his follower. The follower is not letting him lead. It may not be, and usually isn't, deliberate sabotaging on the part of the follower. Perhaps the follower can't follow: his body has not learned to listen to physical instructions. Many things can inhibit that 'listening'—peer pressure, stress, fear… What matters here and now is that in following, they are enabling something to happen, they are sustaining something that will collapse if they stop listening.

Often the leaders are unsuccessful, aggressive, pig-headed. If they give out too many signals, the follower is confused. It is rather like asking someone the way to the Post Office and being given a précis of the entire town grid; it is too much. When aggression takes over, the situation is uneasy. It is no longer a favourite game with a best friend. The audience fear for the follower. The analogy with the relationship between officer and private is all too clear. At the moment, the pair is not able to converse. When a pair in the bamboo-pole game is comfortably holding the pole in the leader/follower scenario, their bodies are conversing. We talk about 'holding' a conversation. It is something that has to be managed in order to succeed.

I work with every pair to bring about comfortable leadership/followership. The others watching are a part of this process. They begin to see for themselves what is blocking the pair in front of them, but instructions belted from their seats are not always helpful. This is something else for them to observe.

I talk about chemistry. In an ideal world we should all be able to get along with each other and work together easily and productively. The bamboo-pole exercise shows again that life is not like that: a couple may be in very great straits. The leader appears to be giving clear physical instructions, he is leading well, it seems. The follower is alert and ready, but somehow the pole keeps on dropping. The couple are simply not 'clicking'. I give the follower a new leader. He now follows easily. A penny has dropped. I now return him to his original partner. Now they work smoothly together. Just the intervention of chemistry was needed. It has been a long morning.

After lunch they are sluggish and comply happily when I suggest they lie on the floor. Ankles cross and snoring begins. I tell them to uncross their ankles. Students hate that, but being alert, even if it means being alert to one's discomfort only, does not happen with ankles crossed. It is like sunbathing with the curtains drawn. I allow them to keep their palms facing the floor. You can't do too much too soon. Now it's time for nursery rhymes. Endless sniggering.

'Take a line from a nursery rhyme you know and sing it as low and as quietly as possible.' Paroxysms of giggles, but they get on with it and ask no questions. 'Is that as low as you can go?' There is a painful silence. Then we play: they experiment with the line—saying it literally, pulling it apart and dragging it over the entire vocal register. The noise is a real jumble of sound. We stop and they sing the line again, but this time surprise themselves by being able to go much lower than before, almost effortlessly. They also feel wide awake and look at me questioningly. We move on. Stand up, in fact.

In groups they prepare a short scene: one has to give orders to the others and the others carry them out. The only text available is the lines from a nursery rhyme of their *individual* choice. They work hard and after fifteen minutes watch each other. Can we understand what is going on? Is it clear? Do those who receive the 'orders' appear to understand? How well did the 'order-giver' do? Did he get aggressive? What happened if he did? Did he lose his authority? In one scene I had to intervene as the order-giver was becoming violent and the others didn't want to continue 'playing'. They were all having to speak a different 'language'. Could they be understood? How many soldiers sent to the Gulf could speak Arabic?

One hour to go, and potentially the most difficult, but usually the most interesting. Feedback. So, what did the group think they got out of the day? Did they discover anything from the work? 'I learned a lot about how I operate with other people', 'I think I'll notice a lot more', 'I discovered so much by just playing.' A lot of agreement mumbling. A few black looks. 'Bloody challenging, Mum. Bloody good thing.' Pause. 'It's the first time we've been honest with each other, and we didn't say anything.' Hurrah for movement! Phew. 'Terrible waste of taxpayer's money, if you ask me, playing *Grandmother's Footsteps*.' Ah… I don't have to respond to this as a lively discussion takes place. Then I compare army training with theatre training; the discipline, the physical endurance, the awareness, the drama. What is the business of an army if not dramatic? But actors don't get killed, so we talk more on the value of a listening body as well as an obeying body. I have infinite respect for them.

The day ends and I receive a very polite 'thank you' letter the following week from the PO in charge. If I have achieved a discussion, even if it is sometimes disturbing, I am satisfied. During my six years of workshops I once played safe: straightforward, textbook stuff, full of teacherly explanation. No one felt like a discussion. I felt I'd failed. Too much explanation, I'm convinced, inhibits learning: too much immediate 'understanding' is limiting.

After a workshop I was always hugely touched by the captains who would thrust mugs of tea into my hand and produce photos of the POs I'd been working with. 'How was he?', 'What about him?' Sometimes I confirmed their worries, or they would sigh, 'We knew you'd like him, but he won't make it, he's too questioning. Thinks too much.'

When the POs have completed their course I always phone to find out how they did and who made it into Sandhurst. There are always one or two surprises. PO Clarke, for example. Just back from Bosnia, his hands perpetually shook. He only had a couple of weeks before returning to the war zone. When we worked, he listened quietly, taking it all in. He was skilful in his handling of his crashing-bore partner; his extraordinary sensitivity carried enormous authority. I felt he was looking me over and thinking, 'Maybe she has just a small something to give us. Let's find a way of getting the best out of her.' Of all people, I felt he would make an excellent officer. Why did he fail? 'He asked the panel questions.' I smiled. The man was clever, had been in combat. Perhaps he knew he just didn't want to be an officer after all.

I treasure my memories of working those six years at Worthy Down, and hope I may work with the armed forces again. Could I call the work 'Movement Play'? Playing, that serious business where the players cannot bear to be interrupted? Where they learn about the world and each other? I'd like to, but no one would buy it, so instead I call it 'Body Language and Communication' or some such. But play is the leveller, the informer and gives the players efficient authority. There exists no real authority that demands obedience over initiative, and that is what my work with the army set out to explore.

In Conclusion

Half an hour to go before a matinée of *David Copperfield*.
It's a LAMDA third-year production and the audience is
dotted about with agents. It's an important time, but the
actors are sluggish. It's that after-lunch 'hopeless' time in
the middle of a run.

'I know, Christian, let's do that nice shoulder-massage
thing you did with us before, and then we could lie
down or something.'

The cast is suddenly all lying down very happily. Poor things!
They need a bit of space.

'Sorry, you are going to walk.' The group walks about. I ask
them not to make eye contact with each other, but to
consider their physical size in the space. What is the distance
between the tops of their heads and the ceiling? Does the
ceiling seem a long way off—or pressing down on them?
How much of themselves do they feel, or is that a tiring or
trying question? Do they feel ready to play? Their bodies are
slow, heavy. They are not quite present; little knapsacks of
personal history are being carried about, comparisons are
being made... Then I ask them to look at the spaces between
each other. In this new space of in-between spaces, the body
finds a new freedom. The mind is engaged on a different
kind of space—there is a new perspective and so more
energy. I then ask them to forget they have a back. They are
'front only', two-dimensional, and are to move as such.

'Consider what 'frontness' means. The front of the
eyes, arms, legs, tongue, etc. How do you sit down

and stand up in frontness? Can you lie on your back in frontness?'

A good ten minutes is spent exploring the freedom, limitations and downright peculiarity of frontness. Then we switch to 'backness'.

'Only move with the back of the body. You have no front. What is the back of the arms, teeth, neck…?'

Another ten minutes in backness, and then snap—no transition—it's frontness again—and then backness again—snap…

'Which is more comfy? Feel the link between the two. Walk about normally, but when I call out 'backness' or 'frontness' be aware of what I am calling on.'

Finally, I ask the actors to return to their 'normal' walk.

Their previous 'normal' and their now 'normal' are miles apart. The group look as though they have grown at least an inch in height and breadth, and I who have been an observer on the outside feel dwarfed.

They are happily surprised. 'Gosh I feel wide awake.' They are awake and alert. The bodies are fully switched on as though a torch has gone on inside them and shone light into the most forgotten places. The body is fully inhabited. It has a sense of its own proportions. It has space. It has perspective. And the group has perspective. Also, the actors are all walking at the same speed. They are in tune with one another. They are a company.

Afterword

And Another Thing...

I called this book *The Space to Move* and I have talked about various aspects of my work. Much I have left out: the place of mask work in actor-training, illusionary mime, bouffon, *Commedia*, work with other cultures, movement training in other countries; but this was not meant to be either a big book or an academic book. What I hope has somehow filtered through from the things I have described is that the space to move and the space to play, whether I was working with actors, children or soldiers were inextricably linked.

If there is no space to move, no space to inhabit, and if there is inside space that is uninhabited, then the body is not functioning as well as it could. By a 'functioning body' I don't mean a 'fit' body that goes to the gym and works out, but one where there is relationship between the parts, relationship with the external space, relationship between mind and body (and a recognition of what does and does not belong to that body), and relationship with its fellows.

It is through play that these relationships develop, it is in play that the body becomes a functioning whole, and it is when the space has been cultivated for play to take place that the 'functioning whole' can be called an actor ready to act. Are these platitudes? Probably, but in my, and so many of my colleagues' experience, they are truths, and delightful ones, at that.

Appendix—Exercises

These are a few of the warm-up and preparatory exercises I use and find particularly useful.

Waking Up the Skin

Cows

1. In pairs, one of you is a prize cow being groomed for a show. Position yourself on your hands and knees with your neck dropped forward and relaxed. Take deep breaths and slowly 'moo' on the out-breath as deeply and softly as you can.

2. Your partner 'grooms' you: using the palms of the hands, your partner rubs your shoulders, back and buttocks using firm, circular movements. Your partner then goes on to brush your spine gently using the flat of the hand to sweep down the spine to the coccyx. Continue to 'moo'.

3. Your partner moves to your arms and legs: they take your arm just below the armpit, between their hands, and roll the flesh from side to side without taking it off the floor, and then move down to the wrist, rolling continuously.

4. Your partner now places a hand gently on your back. Breathe in gently and on the out-breath sing a note or 'moo' into the area under their hand. When the vibration of the sound is felt under the hand, your partner will move his or her hand to another place. See if you can sing into all parts of your back and buttocks.

Waking Up the Feet

Rope

Use a long rope about 1.5cm in diameter and place it taut across the length of the studio floor.

1. With bare feet, stand on the rope and close your eyes.

2. Try to 'tightrope' walk along the rope with your eyes closed.

3. Get off the rope and walk about with your eyes open. Feel the difference in your feet!

This can be done with several people on the rope at the same time. Do this for at least fifteen minutes.

✳

Balls

1. Stand feet parallel, six inches apart. Compare the right and left feet, the right and left arm and place an imaginary spirit-level across the hips and eyes.

2. Place a tennis ball under your right foot and give the foot a good massage by rolling the ball under the entire surface of the foot for at least three minutes. Remember to work it between your toes.

3. Remove the ball and close your eyes. Compare the feet, arms and eyes.

4. Repeat with your left foot.

✳

The Pendulum

Keep the eyes closed and very gently sway from side to side like the pendulum of a clock. Slow and small, keeping the surface of the feet on the ground. Does the body fall more easily to the right or the left? A 'Brain Gym' expert would have reasons for this, but at this stage all that is important is to notice. If a student is asked to understand (or asks to understand) what is happening, then the energy will be blocked and the exercise rendered useless.

Then observe your breathing—is it something that is happening in time to the movement or totally independent of it? Don't change anything—just notice. Then move the body gently forwards and backwards, always keeping the surface of the feet on the ground.

Now, imagining there is a pen sticking out of the top of the head, gently rotate the whole body so the pen can draw a small circle on the ceiling.

Repeat the whole process, making the movements slightly larger. The atmosphere in the studio usually becomes quiet, but only if this exercise is not rushed. Still keeping the eyes closed, come to a standstill. Look at the print of the feet in the mind's eye. Has anything changed?

Most will notice a large change and all reactions will be different. The only useful thing to say is to remind the students that when the clock stops, the pendulum, thanks to gravity, rests perpendicular to the floor. We each have our own perfect perpendicularity, our own perfect posture if you like, but it has to be re-found. The students will now have felt a change, albeit very small. Until they begin to learn to 'feel'—to 'sentir'—in this very small way, they will not know how much there is to feel. This is the very beginning of understanding what it is to be in a group.

∗

The Pendulum (Seated)

Sit on a chair, comfortable, with a sense that you are sitting up straight. Now imagine someone has told you to sit in this position for a two-hour lecture. You might notice that your muscles will contract, you immediately feel a pain in your neck or your knee—it is a pretty ghastly thing to imagine. Now close your eyes and gently sway the body from right to left, the base of your spine through to ten inches above the head moving as one pendulum—small movements back and forth. Now take the movement forwards and backwards and then round in a small circle. All movements are very slow, and see them in the mind's eye whilst doing the exercise.

After a few minutes, stop, open your eyes and notice: you will feel something, however small, has changed. The neck might feel less tense, the body a little more comfortable, the idea of the two-hour lecture may not seem such a nightmare. There will be a difference. Once you begin to notice a change, however small, and feel what is happening in the body, then you are on a road called 'freedom through discovery', because you are just beginning to discover another way the body can work.

∗

Centring

Flipper Feet

1. Stand with your feet parallel, six inches apart, eyes closed.

2. Notice, as in *The Pendulum* exercise, any differences between the two feet. Is one flatter on the ground than the other? Do you lean on one more than the other? Which foot would you stand on for ten minutes if you had to? Do you know? Now place an imaginary ruler across the hips and the line of the eyes. Is the ruler parallel to the floor or does it tilt? Notice.

3. Imagine you have a huge, rubber diver's flipper on your right foot. Now open your eyes and walk about with this right flipper. You have to throw the right leg forward and the 'flipper' slaps the floor. Do not stamp or hit the floor; this is a loud slap and the thigh should wobble a little. The knee is not bent when the leg arrives on the floor. Walk about the room and gradually speed up a little.

4. Stop. Feet parallel again and eyes closed. Compare the two feet and ask yourself the same questions as in the second stage, above. Pay special attention to the line of the eyes. Does one eye feel higher or lower than the other?

5. Repeat using the left leg. Close your eyes and observe the changes.

6. Put two little flippers on and move about as fast as you can. Stop, and without closing the eyes, observe the intensity of the focus.

∗

Balloons in Armpits

1. Walk about the room and consider your size in relation to those around you and the space between yourself and the ceiling.

2. Imagine that in each armpit there is a deflated balloon.

3. Breathing in on the count of five, the balloons inflate, opening the chest and lifting the arms. Walk about the room as you do this. The balloons deflate on the count of five and the chest slumps forward. Let the head drop forward. Keep walking while you inflate and deflate the balloons about ten times.

4. Now inflate the balloons to the count of six: two counts to reach a middle point, two counts in the middle point, two counts to reach super inflation. Two counts to return to the middle point, two counts to stay in the middle point and two to deflate completely. Repeat the process about five times.

5. On the fifth deflation, remain in the middle point and breathe and walk normally. Notice the difference between your original way of walking and this one in relation to the space.

∗

Running

(NB. This exercise should never be done right at the beginning of a session.)

1. In pairs, run around the room in the largest circle possible. Start with your arms lifted high over your head, and your head lifted to gaze at your hands. Shoulders down and sternum lifted.

2. Halfway round the circle the head drops forward (floppy) as do the arms. The body is pitched forward, but the running continues at the same pace. Take care to keep the head relaxed.

3. When the circle has been completed, return to the first stage. There is no middle state between the first and second stages.

4. After each pair has completed the circle four or five times, go from the 'high state' to your normal run. Notice how you can continue running

indefinitely, and also notice that not only are you running in step with your partner but that the whole group is running in step. (One of my students at LAMDA, always apologetic and angry at his, as he saw it, lack of athleticism, carried on running for fifteen minutes after this exercise, giving us the speech he had had to prepare for his voice class: clear, open and with no hint of breathlessness.)

Grounding: Bringing the Centre Down

Trees

This is a very easy exercise and delightful to do with children as well as adults.

1. Stand with your feet parallel, about twelve inches apart. Ask a partner to see if they can lift you off the floor an inch or two.

2. Now, alone, and with the eyes shut, imagine you have roots growing through your legs and feet down into the earth to a depth of about ten feet. Imagine the roots curling tightly round a huge anchor deep in the earth. Take your time.

3. Open your eyes and ask your partner to try and lift you again. Ask the largest person in the room to lift you!

Bums to the Sky

1. Walk about the room and notice where you feel your centre to be. Do not try to be logical: you may feel your centre is outside you somewhere.

2. With your feet parallel, bend your knees and let the body hang over them, head and arms relaxed. Check your knees are directly above your toes and not falling in towards each other.

3. Imagine there is a little face on the sacrum (the large, triangular bone at the base of the spine) which wants to look up at the sky.

4. Breathe in, and on the out-breath lift the 'face' skyward by gently straightening the legs. The point is not so much to straighten your legs as to lift the face. Bend the legs when you need to breathe in again. Repeat very slowly about six times.

5. On an out-breath uncurl the spine slowly to stand. Observe where your centre is now.

The Feldenkrais Leg-drop

1. Lie on your back with your knees drawn up and your feet planted on the floor, the width of your hips apart.

2. Pull the trouser on your left thigh towards you to pull the foot off the floor.

3. Let go of the trouser and let your foot fall back to the floor. Notice the noise it makes, the feel of the fall. Try it on the right and compare.

4. Both feet on the floor, make circular movements with the ball of the left foot on the floor where it lies, pushing hard into the ground. Now increase the movement, so you work all round the foot, pushing your toes, then the outside of your foot, then your heel, then your instep, into the floor in slow circular movements. Now rock the foot between heel and toe.

5. Rest. Now lift the trouser of the left thigh again, pulling the foot off the floor. Let it drop as before and notice the quality of the sound on the floor and compare it with the right foot.

6. Come up to stand very slowly and take a walk. Compare right and left feet.

7. Repeat the process with your right leg.

The Walk

1. Walk around the room.

2. Gradually engage the balls of your feet so you are rolling through the feet to the toes.

3. Use the balls of your feet as springboards, push-off points.

4. Notice any change in your eyes and your focus.

5. Keep pushing off the balls of your feet until you spontaneously break into a little trot. Keep pushing off until you are leaping across the room.

6. Now walk engaging the heels only. Notice what happens in your sternum and your eyes.

7. Return to pushing off from the balls of the feet. Notice the tiny lift in your sternum. Alternate heel walk with 'push-off' walk.

8. Return to your 'normal' walk. What has happened? By going to extremes you will have re-found your true centre and everyone will be walking at the same speed: clear, ready, no baggage.

On Working with Christian...

Richard Armitage

There are many of Christian's techniques which I still use for my character studies, vocal work and preparation for performance, whether it's on television, radio or stage.

I regularly use animal study to seek out an inner character. I remember when Christian took our human zoo for an outing to Regent's Park. I really quite believed I was a tamarin monkey and that branches in trees would support my weight. They didn't!

Christian took care of the very fine details; and was inspiring for a bunch of overenthusiastic drama students who crashed in on day one of the first term, just wanting to 'act the face off everything'. I feel I ended my three years with a physical vocabulary which was highly sensitive and expressive, and sustainable through a career of varying characters and media.

Something that Christian said to me has served as a mantra ever since. Whilst studying the Seven States of Tension, we were set an exercise to devise an original movement piece involving all of the Seven States, but not more than five minutes long. I spent hours editing Orff's *Carmina Burana* to bring it in at exactly five minutes, to accompany my piece incorporating all the qualities. With my stopwatch in constant use, I finally had a piece that matched the criteria. When it came to performing our pieces, other members of the class began extending over the five-minute time limit; five, ten, twenty seconds over... I was appalled and, after performing my piece, was very unsatisfied as it so clearly lacked something.

'Had you taken a few extra moments with this, this and this,' Christian explained, 'it would have been lovely.'

'But, Christian, that would have taken me over five minutes!'

She laughed. 'Well, Richard, it is good sometimes to be a little anarchic and break the rules to find what you want.'

I have carried that with me ever since.

Samuel Barnett

I had danced for ten years before going to drama school, and I feared I had a lot of bad habits to undo. I felt very held in my body from all the ballet work I had done; I could only work from the neck up and was not fully in touch with myself. Working with Christian I began to discover things about myself—in terms of my body and my physical movement, as well as my acting—that I didn't know I had inside me. That was always the way with her classes, whatever we were doing, and the work opened me up as an actor. I learned how to express myself through my whole body. I learned the meaning of 'a sense of timing': if I could sense when to move at just the right moment in an exercise or movement piece, I could also learn how to time the delivery of a line perfectly.

Christian showed us the value of movement to acting. Many of the group at LAMDA had perhaps not been interested in movement or dance of any sort before, but her classes were relevant to actor training by showing how to investigate character from a physical perspective, instead of just the emotional, intellectual and psychological elements, where a lot of actors stay stuck. Sometimes working from the outside in can produce the best, most revealing work—much more quickly. I can't say what it's like to be an old man. But if I imagine and change my physicality then I might begin to feel it far more effectively than if I analyse it emotionally and intellectually. Then you can make a true transformation where people say, 'I really didn't see you in there anywhere.'

Since leaving LAMDA, many of my acting roles have required me to move, especially Philip Pullman's *His Dark Materials* at the National Theatre, in which I had to convey my entire physical and emotional self through a puppet. Without Christian's classes I wouldn't have known how to begin.

Dominic Cooper

I never admitted to Christian that the 'smelly dog' that she thought I imitated with such perfection was actually meant to be a lion. I loved Christian and her magical classes. She was like a delicate sparrow tiptoeing around the dilapidated, mirrored rehearsal room, whispering words of inspiration. She created a calm and serene environment that gave us all the confidence to take risks—but ultimately enjoy what is essentially lots of fun. I always think of her smile and her excitement when a student realised in themselves the potency and effect our physicality on stage has on an audience.

Félicité du Jeu

As a teacher and as a person, Christian had an ability to expand people's vision. Theatre is the work and result of many. She embraced that idea fully. Softly yet firmly, she'd push any believed limit a little further, a little more towards giving, a little more towards the unsuspected. All her teaching was based on the ripple effect of any given interaction. Movement is life's answer back to nought; it bares our inner clock, our inner souls. For Christian, that's where the actor's work started, that first impulse triggering a physical chain effect. It was the actor's job to seek out those first truthful movements. The rest would follow. Joy, dedication, precision and finally fulfilment were always in reach in Christian's classes.

Index

Games and exercises are indicated in bold

à l'écoute   13–18, 95
aerobics   164
Aeschylus (*Persai*)   14–15
Alexander Technique   29–31
Alert Stillness   66–7
l'Ange qui dérange
   /Disturbing angel
   113–15
Animal Dynamics   66
Animal, Into the   69–71
animal work   59–79
animalité   60–62, 76, 77
Antennes d'Escargot   67–8
Aristophanes (*Birds*)   72
army, working with   108,
   169–76
Assisted Breathing   26, 63–6
auto-contact   136–140
**Auto-contact Movements and
   Musicality**   136–138
awareness   3, 23
Awareness Through Movement
   (ATM)   30

backness and frontness
   177–8
Ball', 'I Throw You the   54–7,
   172
Balloons in Armpits   11–12,
   183
Balls   181
Bamboo Poles   171–4
Birds   71
Birds (Aristophanes)   72
body space (relaxation)   24–6
Breast Versus Chest   88–90

breath/breathing   19, 61–2, 70,
   106
Breathing   62
Breathing, Assisted   63–6
Breathing, Steam-   27–8
**Breathing exercises/
   techniques**   11, 26–8,
   62–6, 182
Bridgmont, Peter   117
Bums to the Sky   184
Butterfly Effect, the   133–4

carrier/the carried, the (*le porteur
   /le porté*)   96–8
Centring exercises   10–12, 40,
   182–3
Chest Versus Breast   88–92
children, working with   82–3,
   91, 159–68
Children, games enjoyed by
   50–51, 54–5, 67–8, 184
choreography   124–5, 134
chorus   16–17, 72, 140
company   1–2, 160, 178
Contact exercises   85, 86,
   88–90
contact work   80–99
Cows   86, 180

Decroux, Étienne   53, 59, 60,
   67, 81, 99, 134, 145, 147,
   150
Disturbing angel/*l'Ange qui
   dérange*   113–15
Dubois, Catherine   60, 96–7

écouter 3
l'écoute, être à 13–18, 95
élan 55–8, 105–7, 109–11
ensemble 6–7
Euripides (*Iphigeneia in Aulis*) 16
Eyes-closed exercises 26, 85–6, 88–90, 93–8

Feldenkrais Leg-drop, The 38, 185
Feldenkrais Method 29–31
Feldenkrais, Moshe 23
Flipper Feet 10, 38, 182
focus 54–7, 112
follower/leader 86–7, 142–3, 172–4
Following and Leading 125–8
Football and Watch-mending 111–12
frontness and backness 177–8
Fulguration 67
Fulkerson, Mary 80

Gaulier, Philippe 25, 54, 106, 111
Grandmother's Footsteps 50–52, 171
Groggy Space 26–7
group 6, 9, 17, 20, 93, 156

Hannaford, Carla 83
Heggen, Claire 60

improvisation 29, 32, 46, 54, 77, 114, 146–9
intention 52–3, 104, 107, 112, 120, 124, 135
Into the Animal 69–71
Iphigeneia in Aulis (Euripides) 16
'I Throw You the Ball' 54–8, 172

Johnstone, Keith 54, 148

Knee Circles 22–3

Laban, Rudolf 134
Leading and Following 125–8
leader/follower 86–7, 142–3, 172–4
leadership (army) 170, 172, 173
Lecoq, Jacques 31
Lecoq's Seven States of Tension 31–49
Lecoq's Raft 131
Leg-drop, The Feldenkrais 38, 185
Lettre au Porteur (Théâtre du Mouvement) 95–9
listening 3–4, 13–18, 99, 140, 142, 171–4

Making Contact 85
Marc, Yves 60
mask 119, 151
Midsummer Night's Dream, A (Shakespeare) 124, 129
movement and voice 104–5
movement training 2–3, 113
Murray, Jan 80
music 145–6
musicality 3, 12–18, 124–44

noise 108–9
notice/noticing 3–4, 8–10, 23, 30, 170

objects 146–55

Pagneux, Monika 8, 25, 171
Pardo, Enrique 113, 125, 128, 142
pastoral care 156–7
Paxton, Steve 80
Pendulum, The 9–10, 32, 181–2
Pendulum, The (Seated) 30, 182
performance 54, 130, 146
Persai (Aeschylus) 14–15
physical theatre 160

play   2, 13, 50–58, 76–7, 104,
   108, 110–12, 116–17, 123,
   132, 151–2, 159, 160–64, 176,
   179
point of suspension   55–8
porteur/ le porté, le (the carrier/the
   carried)   96–8
posture   9, 65
props   144–55

Raft (Lecoq's)   131
rehearsal   1, 78, 105, 125, 145–6,
   150, 155
relaxation   19–28, 106, 156
Relaxation exercises   22–3,
   26–8
**Relaxation (*l'Ange qui
   dérange*)**   113–15
repetition   166
resonance   34–5, 108–9, 134,
   139–43
Retallack, John   124
rhythm   144, 151
Rigoletto (Verdi)   16
Rodenburg, Patsy   21
role   12, 158, 161–2
Rope   180
Running   11–12, 183–4

Seven States of Tension   31–49
   State One   33–6, 46–7,
   48–9
   State Two   37–9, 46–7,
   48–9
   State Three   39–40, 46–7,
   48–9
   State Four   40–42, 46–7,
   48–9
   State Five   42–3, 46–7, 48–9
   State Six   43, 46–7, 48–9
   State Seven   44–5, 46–7,
   48–9
**Seven States of Tension,
   Playing with the**   46–7
Shakespeare, William (*A
   Midsummer Night's Dream*)
   124, 129

shock and resonance   139–42
Shock and Resonance
   140–2
soldier   50, 109–10, 169–70
space/spacing   7–8, 124–36
Stanislavsky, Konstantin   122
Steam-breathing   27–8
Stillness   35, 45, 53, 107, 117,
   132
Stillness, Alert   66–7
story   53, 143, 164–6
suspension   50–58, 134

technique   6–7, 26, 102, 166,
   172
technique, getting the best out of
   28–49
technique, voice   100–123
tension   31, 44, 116
Tension, Seven States of
   31–49
text   55–8, 113–23, 125, 158
Théâtre du Mouvement   60, 96
Theatre for Africa   60–61
Thiery, Lucas   96
timing   98, 130, 140
touch   82–5, 91
training   1–3, 6, 19–20, 25, 29,
   31, 54, 78, 81–2, 104, 113,
   118, 156–8, 170, 175
transformation   59–61, 73, 78
Trees   184
trust   26, 80, 92–5
Trust exercises   26, 85–6,
   88–90, 93–8
typecasting   158

Verdi, Giuseppe (*Rigoletto*)   16
visual spacing   124–44
Visual Spacing exercises
   125–8, 131–2, 136–8, 140–42
voice   100–123

Waking Up the Feet exercises
   180–2
Waking Up the Skin exercises
   86, 180

Walk, The   40, 185
warm-up   5, 32, 180
Watch-mending and Football
   111–12
Way of Doing (WOD)   113–16,
   120, 122
workshop   1, 159, 160, 167, 170,
   175
Wrestling   44–5

'Yes!' Exercise, The   109–10